THE ONE LAW

for Amazing Abundance
in Every Area of Your Life

.

THE ONE LAW

for Amazing Abundance
in Every Area of Your Life

Marjah Simon-Meinefeld, Esq.

THE ONE LAW

for Amazing Abundance in Every Area of Your Life

© 2020 Marjah Simon-Meinefeld, Esq.

ISBN: 9798630919687 Paperback

The strategies in this book are presented for educational and entertainment purposes. All quotes remain the proprietary property of the authors. Every effort has been made to trace copyright holders and obtain permission for the use of copyright material where applicable.

The information and resources presented are based on the author's personal opinion. Any outcome or results vary with each individual. There is no guarantee as to the results.

The author reserves all rights to make changes and assumes no responsibility or liability on behalf of any purchaser, reader or user of these materials.

For complimentary templates to accompany the life transformation steps in this book, while available, visit www.AWA4Life.com.

DEDICATIONS

I dedicate this book first and foremost back to the Source from which it came. Thank You God for flowing through me. Thank You for blessing me abundantly so that I can be a continual source of blessings for others. I thank You for guiding me (sometimes with a strong shove) in the path of my highest self.

As I grow and evolve through the rest of my life, I thank You now. I count it all as good.

I want to express my deepest gratitude to my mother Geneva, my father Clive, and to all my ancestors: Thank you for your life experiences – and the lessons you learned. Because you loved me, I believe I am now the best of who you were.

I tap into the daily flow of your wisdom, your joy and your love. It helps me to understand more deeply, to forgive more quickly, and to grow more purposely.

And finally, **I dedicate this book to you, the readers.** It is your readiness to receive this One Law which produced the flow of words that make up this writing.

Because of your open heart, the Universe poured its words through me for you. Thank you for allowing me to be the vessel. I love you.

ACKNOWLEDGEMENTS

Sending special thanks to:

Marcus, my patient husband, thank you for choosing every day to love me and for filling my life with song.

My daughters Jada and Alejandra, from the moments you chose me to be your mother, I've been on fire to change the world, just so it can be more amazing for you. You are my muses, my biggest reasons why, and my heartbeat.

My dear siblings, Jasmine, Kintu, Kai, we know where we came from, and why we are becoming, doing, and giving. Thank you for sharing this life journey with me.

My grandson Alex, my nieces Sonia and Savanah, my nephew J. Adrian, you are my next generation that inspires me to create Generational Wealth in self-care, relationships, money and health, so that you may freely choose to live in your gifts and experience the One Law every day. This is my hope for you.

My chosen family - my friends Tracie M, Renae B, Annabelle B, René D, Balbinder D, Gideon B, Jasmin

M, Markus W, MeShell B, Monica H, Jeanette R., Monique B , Liz H, Christina B, Francesca A, Dhivya O, Osvaldo T, all my Inner Heart family, my Platinum family, and the many more hearts I'm connected with through Tony Robbins' events, Toastmasters International, Heidelberg Int'l Professional Women's Forum, Bethel Community Church International of Tinton Falls NJ, Zeta Phi Beta Sorority Inc, Phi Beta Sigma Fraternity Inc, and all of the Divine 9, and my neighbors that make my house feel like home - you've all enriched my life, encouraged, challenged, supported, laughed and cried with me. And we've often laughed so hard until we cried...life is great.

Bishop and Lady Blacknall, my spiritual parents, thank you for your constant prayers, encouragement and belief in me as I fulfill what God has for me to do.

Tony Robbins, you taught me how to see things as they are, then see them better than they are, and then create it. Thank you for your wisdom in coaching me to stay connected to my heart for helping.

Joseph McClendon III, your caring coaching helped me to see the possibilities through the pain, where I could take the steps to change my life. What an incredible difference!

Luke Wren, thank you for teaching me to focus on my next step, for giving me guidance and encouragement when I feel stuck and for celebrating with me. Your heart for people is genuine, and I am genuinely grateful.

Mandy Schumaker, we've haven't met face to face, yet you get me. I love that there's no BS'ing you. Your insight, accountability, and determination that I live up to my potential keeps me moving forward every day.

Chloë Bisson, Alex, Kristine and the whole amazing team, you are the reason this book went from my computer to the world, and can now change lives. Professionalism at its finest.

Table of Contents

PROLOGUE

It may seem a strange thing for a writer to admit to, but I didn't write the first section of this book. Not in the traditional sense anyway.

This book began creating itself on June 11, 2017. I was woken up out of my sleep at about 3 am to the words forming in my head. It was so insistent that I got out of bed in search of pen and paper to capture it. And the words flowed from its Source through me, down my pen and onto the paper for over an hour.

This ritual was repeated off and on for about two weeks, and always around 3 am – 5 am. It became so routine that I joked around about my lack of sleep not being a concern, as long as the book got written.
But then I read all of what was written. I will be transparent with you – I was afraid.

I was afraid of the words and what they revealed. I was afraid to put my name on it and present it to the world. But I could feel the purity through which it flowed. Still, I hid it away on my computer for 2 ½ years. Until now. There was a small whisper now gently commanding one thing "It's time". And I couldn't ignore it any more. After all, they were not my words to decide to keep.

This book is a gift for the world to light the path on your personal and collective enlightenment journey.

As an empath, I've learned over the decades to be comfortable with being uncomfortable with how I receive information. I can feel the true, often hidden emotions of people, which can be a lot of energies and information to process.

I also sometimes see the future in dreams and visions, which began when I was 12 years old. The information I receive through dreams and visions used to scare me when I'd see things come true. I'd have a very vivid, specific type of dream. Then the next day, or a few days later, I'd see it happen, just as I dreamt.

Like any child without guidance or context, I felt like a freak of nature. So, I began intentionally ignoring the visions and trying to forget the dreams by singing obnoxiously loud, with my fingers in my ears and my eyes shut. After a while, the dreams and visions came less and less frequently, and I'd forget more and more. Or maybe I was just more disconnected from them.

A few weeks later, I went to a family barbeque at my uncle's house in Long Island NY. The entire family was in the backyard having a great time. I was sitting in the living room alone watching tv. The front door opened and a woman that I had never seen before walked in. Just when she got a few steps past me, she stopped, turned and stared at me until I diverted my gaze from the tv to her.

She said knowingly "You've got a very special gift. It's here to help you and to help others. But if you keep pushing it away, it will eventually go away completely. You don't have to be afraid. It's something to be treasured and appreciated. I urge you to accept it and use it. You are safe and protected. It's ok." And with that, she continued walking towards the backdoor towards the yard. I sat there stunned.

I had never told anyone about any of this – not the dreams, or visions, and certainly not about my intentionally trying to make them stop. I felt strangely relieved that someone knew and that I was ok. I got up off the couch and walked to the back yard. She was not there. And I never saw her again. I believe it was a visit from an angel sent to guide me and to free me from fear surrounding the gifts I was experiencing.

To all of the other empaths who may be hiding your gifts, please know that there is nothing wrong with you. The world needs you to be brave and stand up and own who you are. Learn to protect yourself and not to absorb the sometimes overwhelming energy that you are feeling. I've learned to be aware and tune into it, without allowing it to consume me. This balance is important to do what we do effectively.

Over the decades, I have been privileged to communicate information that helped many people to avoid challenges and disasters. But even then, I only told people when it was really necessary where the information came from.

Now I've grown accustomed to sharing this part of myself more freely with people. It's as natural to me as the color of my eyes or my height. However, this is the very first time I am openly talking about this with all of you. I guess "it's time" to also be open about this.

Please understand, this is nothing I control. I do not seek these dreams and visions out. They come when they come, and I'm then often given instructions on who to deliver the potential future information to.

People have the choice at that point as to change their decisions to alter course or not. I've learned that my whole job is to be the messenger and deliver the opportunity.

What they do with it is up to them. We all have free will. I believe that if our Universal Source, which I call God, provides me with this information about future events, it is because there are moments where we are being urged to shift in a different direction.

Sometimes I see things only after they occur so that I can prepare myself when I come face to face with it, or to give me insight to help someone with specifically what they need.

I believe that the events that are only revealed to me after the occurrence is because it was not an event to be altered. It was just so I can show up in full compassion and understanding.

I've learned to be ok with all of it, no matter the outcome. I am grateful to be trusted with such a role in humanity. It's enabled me to have more compassion and understanding without judgement. I see the innocence in all of us, and I honor you. I've written ideas and stories that have come to me through dreams in the past.

But this book is the only time that I can recall entire chapters flowing out completed. And this was the only time for it to be on such a topic.

Some people may not believe anything I just shared. Some may dismiss what I've written down in this book. But I'm ok with that. Like I said, we all have free will.

We each must be ready, in our own time, to receive and understand certain wisdoms. So, if this book helps you today, next year, or 5 years from now, I trust that it will be in the exact right moment for you. Whenever it may be, thank you for allowing the words that I've been given to have a space in your precious life. Even if you don't believe in the underlying reasons that I share in this book, I urge you to still be open to doing the exercises that follow about transforming into the best version of you. Because it works.

You'll see your life shift in amazing ways, and all the world will be better for it.

With all the loving light of the universe to you,
Marjah

INTRODUCTION

What is the One Law? What is this law through which all other laws of the universe flow through?

If I tell you now, you might not believe me. So, I'll share with you what was revealed to me, as I heard it.

In reading the first section of this book, you will realize this special law for yourself. In this discovery, you'll have the option of internalizing it, and living it intentionally and abundantly.

Life will hold a sweetness like you've never known before. Colors will dance in your eyes more vividly. Music will caress your ears, and your heart more deeply. The scent of life will be like fresh bread out of the oven.

You'll feel a connective flow so powerful that your life will never be the same again. This is a lofty promise. But it's not my promise. It is the result of remembering your rights and your responsibilities in the One Law, and then living the law consistently.

I urge you to re-read the first section of this book before reading and applying each of the subsequent five chapters. This will help you to discover the One Law faster, and to apply it to the steps you are taking in your transformative abundance journey.

We are on this amazing odyssey together. Get excited! Life is opening up to deliver you everything your heart desires.

We've, as a race of humans, traversed many ages of living, including the agricultural age, the industrial age, and now the informational age. We have never before had so much information and so little wisdom.

What will become of the human race? Death? Extinction? No. Death is an illusion. There is only a change in the state in which life exists. But there is a new void in the world today. Nature abhors a void.

The void many are experiencing is a forgetting of wisdom directing us to love, to forgive, to cherish, to help, to hope, to care. This void however is also ushering in the new age – the Age of Enlightenment. In the contrast, more of us are waking up, remembering who we really are.

Living from the heart will be the new normal. Loving the loveless, forgiving the unforgivable, and trusting the Unseen will be the currencies that brings mankind their treasures. The light within will lead each to his or her true purpose. Each will accept and live in this purpose, bringing through them their special shade and color of light into this world.

As more people accept the Age of Enlightenment, balance and harmony will be restored to the world.

Abundance shall replace lack, which is only an illusion anyway.

Where there is doubt, it will be replaced by faith. The despairs and pains of life will speedily give way to hope of a better moment, and gratefulness for all experiences.

Understanding shall replace ignorance. The realization that we, the entire world, are one collective organism, will become as factually clear and accepted as the Earth being round rather than flat. We will understand the One Law in this New Age. And we will realize that any harm we do to another, we do to ourselves.

How can we cut off our own arm and not injure the hand? How can we pluck out our eye and keep our vision?

In this Age of Enlightenment, we will see tomorrow and yesterday within our today, and also understand the illusion of time, as well as the truth of why we use the illusion. Time provides us with a vehicle with which to measure how close or far we are moving to our Enlightenment. It's so we have a sense of urgency in this important life or "death" matter of realizing the One Law.

To become our highest self, to have such abundance that the overflow feeds the world, is why we exist. The oneness of the organism that we are, requires of itself growth. It is only in growth that the fullness of the Source of All is realized.

This cannot be understood in the head, but only in the 1st organ, the heart. Each heartbeat in each living creature is a note in a great symphony. This music is what God rejoices in.

The oneness of us originated in the Source of All. In the Age of Enlightenment, we are going home. We are "reconnecting" permanently, by realizing the One Law.

Right now, many of us tap in and tap out like a flickering street light. But soon, the light in us will burn bright, and illuminate the way for others to also follow their true purpose for being. The only reason for the darkness is so we can seek and choose to live in the light. It is in finally making the choice that we begin to truly live, not just make a living.

As this message flows into the world, many may not be ready. But those that are ready, will lead the way into the New Age of Enlightenment. Enlightenment:

"Into the light with purposeful love" is the new definition.

As those that are now ready hear this message, your heart will reveal your purposeful love – the reasons for your creation, and the meaning of your life. Listen. You will know in your heart who you truly are, and see the falsehood of any other life you may be living.

You will be emboldened with faith to step from the false into the full truth of who you really are.

No voice of unbelievers, nor their fears, will be able to stop you. The peace of God will enable you to take the bold step into your highest self. And I thank you for doing so. As each of us fully embrace who we really are, and do something bold about living it, your energy from Source will no longer trickle, but rather flow through us, filling us, and spilling over.

The thirst for what is real will finally be quenched. A very few have already begun entering this Age and are lovingly lighting the way for you. Seek them and you will find them sharing their insights. Your heart will guide you and you'll know they are the real ones. This is not a religion so do not be fooled. You do not need to follow any other human being as "higher" than you. We are all one. This is not magic or mystical.

Do the heart work as you do the hard work. This journey is not an easy one, but it is worth it. It is the only thing that is worth your life, your breath, your heartbeat.

You may have to release things you once thought were valuable or important to walk this journey. But in release, abundance in every area of your life will flow to you. God rejoices in your abundance of love, health, relationships, money, peace, and every other area of your life's desires.

This is true wealth.

In your life of purpose, all is open to you. It is open to you now, only you may not be in the right place to receive it. If I bury the Hope Diamond by the ocean, tell you where it is buried so that you may dig it up and be rich, but instead, you dig by the lake, will you ever unearth your diamond?

Too much of life has been spent digging by the quiet, small lake. It may be comforting and familiar, but it will never provide you the freedom awaiting you by the ocean. Yes, the ocean is bigger and scarier. But true purpose is like that. And as you do the heart work and the hard work of learning how to swim in your special gift, the ocean of purposeful living will become your refuge. It will no longer feel as scary, but rather exciting.

Everything you need will appear as you need it. It must, because you are finally digging in the right place, where your Hope has been buried. You are bestowed with a purpose. Stop doubting yourself and your abilities. Begin to trust your heart instead.

Instincts are your heart's way of communicating truths while you are awake, truth your head can't see or reason its way through. While asleep, dreams are the way your heart connects your current river to your ocean of possibilities. In Dream-state, we are finally quiet, open, and listening. Our heart has control, and turns that control over to our Source of All.

Our purpose, our reasons for being, is revealed, layer by layer. The plans for our life are laid out clearly. For The Source of All knows the plans and reveals them to all who are ready to hear them and receive them. We then are commanded to act upon them.

Unfortunately, so many right now, never admit to themselves that they already know the plan for their life that has been revealed. It may not be popular, or sexy, or easy. So, it is ignored. It is, I am sure, well outside of your comfort zone. Therefore, many pretend that they never received the message. And even those of us that admit we received the message of our life's purpose, we reject it rather than receive it. We reject it with words of doubt, fear, ridicule, and the act of inaction.

We misuse our minds with destructive thoughts. We tell ourselves that we are not good enough, not ready enough, not worthy enough, not able enough, not _____ enough (fill in the blank with your own disempowering words), and that we will fail and then no longer be loved. Or we tell ourselves that if we succeed, we will become different, get rejected by those that know us as we are now, and then we will no longer be loved. Or we tell ourselves that the world will find out we are a fraud, not to be believed, and reject us, and we will no longer be loved.

Entering the Age of Enlightenment requires the understanding that we can never NOT be loved. The Source of All, the Light which created us, is Love.

Love is the substance that we are created from and the energy we are connected to which keeps our heart beating.

We are rejected because we reject ourselves. Remember now. We are one organism. As we grow in the faith of our purpose, and walk in that purpose, love realized will also grow in abundance. And the light of love that you are becoming radiates, it will overtake the darkness of "not enough love". This illusion will become less and less a part of your existence.

Once you accept the fact that when you live in your divinely created purpose, you can only be connected to the truth of love, the fears that may now be holding you back will no longer have power over you. These fears gather their power through the wrong thoughts we entertain and dwell on in our minds.

In the Age of Enlightenment, the purpose of your mind will no longer primarily be to confuse you with conflicting thoughts, but to house constructive thoughts that entice you to act in alignment with your true purpose. This too, may not always be easy.

Learning to allow thoughts to flow through us rather than holding it as a blockage requires practice, so most

16

might not be willing to do it. But it is critical in entering the Age of Enlightenment. We truly are creating what we consistently, emotionally think about.

{At this point in the revealing of this information through me, I felt exhausted suddenly, as if released from the flow of it all temporarily. I was given permission to sleep.

It was nearly 3 am. God normally woke me up between 3:30 and 4:30 am to talk with me. I begged that if this were the case this morning, to please put my body and mind supernaturally into a state of refreshed sleep. I set my alarm, with hope for some sleep, for 7:04 am.

I had a dream where information was revealed to me. At 7 am exactly my eyes opened. Awake, I was given instructions to write down the dream here.}

There is a couple - a man and a woman. They have two sons. They used to have another son, but he has passed on. That son, in my dream, they kept calling "Fo". I don't know if that was a nickname or a part of the name I was able to understand in the dream. There was also a medium to big sized dog.

As the family relayed the story to me of Fo's death (which I don't remember), one of the "boys" (they were grown men as well), put on a cap of some sort and a white t-shirt that belonged to Fo. The dog, which up until then seemed to be very calm and disinterested, began to bark and jump excitedly on the guy wearing Fo's clothes. He pawed at him, as if attempting to reach the man he so loved, as if someone he loved dearly was suddenly there.

The family revealed that this dog had belonged to Fo. I told them that the dog was their key to healing. Fo is still in communication with his dog, and he is with them and wants them to heal and be at peace, just as the dog is at peace. The dog's peace comes from the knowing that Fo is still alive, as spirit. Fo wants his family to know it too, and begin the process of healing.

Before writing this dream down, I asked the Originator of the dream to reveal to me who this family is. I don't know if I will meet them before or after this is published, or if at all, but I do know that they will see this message.

My prayer is that Fo's message will soothe their souls, and release them from the pain dwelling deep inside that family. One of the family members is ready now to enter the Age of Enlightenment. In healing from this experience, that person will be able to do so, and help guide the others.

Out of the pouring storms of tragedy, when we are ready, comes rainbows. Rainbows are a refraction of colors, revealed usually in an arch, like a bridge. I believe since the beginning of time people have been trying to find the ends of the natural rainbows when they appear. But as they approach it, it seems to move just out of their vision and reach. It is because we cannot reach the ends of the rainbows naturally, but only supernaturally, through our hearts.

At one end of the rainbow is the river we may have chosen to dig by, and feeling as if we are barely living. At the other end of the rainbow is our vast ocean of purposeful lives being lived. From the river to the ocean is a bridge of colorful light. The colors represent the many, many purposes that are placed into each and every beating heart.

We have been given the choice to walk across that bridge, in the color or colors of our choosing. This is how we find our treasure, our "pot of gold" at the end of the rainbow that so many fairy tales and stories speak of. "Where your heart is, there your treasure will be also". This is how we manifest the un-stealable treasure of heaven on earth.

Every dream you obtain has an impact far greater than you can imagine.

In in-purpose living, our collective consciousness, the Oneness that we are, is synchronized once again. The Age of Enlightenment is the gateway to this synchronicity. A new way is emerging. And it depends on each one of us to walk our part of the grand design. If we choose not to, it will happen anyway, but without you experiencing who you really are. And we will all feel that, because we are one.

As an individual, we are in a delusion of separateness. It is only when this so called "individual" becomes their highest self, do they emerge from this delusion of separateness, and into the reality of Source. We are one, came from One and, in this New Age, are finding our way back. We are finding our way back to the memory that we've chosen to forget – that we are still, and always will be One.

Listen to that still, quiet voice inside of you. It is the Oneness guiding you back to your true self. Don't let the noise of the world, which is in the delusion of separateness, keep you afraid.

When you fully embrace the wonderfulness of who you really are and do something bold about living it, there is only love, no more fear of lovelessness.

There is light, not darkness. There is joy, not sadness. There is faith, not doubt. There is forgiveness, not injury.

When we sow into the world, the reality of who we were designed to be, we reap abundance. This abundance overflows to all throughout eternity. And because we are one, it flows back to you again. This is what it is to experience heaven. Heaven is not simply a place, it is a state of being Source – of being love, of being the real you.

You may be afraid now because you are seeing the separateness, and believing the lie that you aren't or won't be loved. Again, this is an impossibility. You come from pure love, without condition, without reservation, and without end.

When in fear or doubt or confusion, pray. Prayer is a universal request. "Where two or more are gathered, there I will be in the midst of them." The "two or more" means an understanding of togetherness, of oneness. It's an act in faith, of coming out of separateness and into the One that we are.

Prayer releases the floodgates that we've bottled up with disbelief and doubt. Once released, faith words, which are prayers in motion, are creating more of the Universe. *Uni*-meaning "one", and *verse*- meaning "a writing arranged with a metrical rhythm" is where we live. We are created with one word, and that word is <u>always</u> LOVE.

In the One Law we are hearing and moving in that rhythm. In that rhythm, abundance flows through every area of our lives.

{When my eldest daughter Jada was about 3 years old, she came to me and said,

"I'm so glad I picked you to be my mommy." I asked, "What do you mean?" She replied in her childlike purity, "I was walking with God in heaven and saw you. I asked God if you could be my mommy. And God said "Yes".

"I was stunned. I asked her, "You remember heaven?" "Of course", she replied. "Can I ask you a question?"
"Yes."
"What is the meaning of life?" Without hesitation Jada replied,
"Love".

She looked at me in confusion as to why I would ask her such an 'obvious' question. I think she said "Duh" as she toddlered off, completely unaware of the perfectness and clarity with which she answered a question that has seemed to plague mankind for all eternity.

She remembered heaven!

She remembered being in Oneness, walking and talking with the Source. And it was obvious fact to her that we are alive to express ourselves in love.}

The only way we fully are able to express ourselves in love, is to fully express ourselves in love – our true selves. Be who you are created to be in love and in truth, and in so doing, you tap into your Source of creating. You release your power to manifest and grow the Universe.

Your word - the one that created the beauty and purpose within you, is waiting to be spoken. But only you can speak it. Others may have the same word (purpose) but only you can speak that word with your voice. You will find many ways (just as there are many rainbow colors reflected) in which you will express that word.

Manifestor, we are waiting for you to be brave. We love you, and always will. Believe and speak your word. Live your purpose fully to express love to all the world.

There are signs everywhere on your journey. When we are going in the direction of our destiny, we are in flow, and we will see supportive, encouraging signs. They are directing and leading you to your highest self. These signs are often ignored, at our detriment. Ignoring the signs slows our journey and increases our suffering. But, the more you look, the more you will see.

{Signs may come through numbers appearing repeatedly in our path. For me, multiples of the number 4 are repeated when I am on the right path. I see it on license plates of cars driving in front of me, on highway signs, on the sides of taxis, on billboards, on receipts, and even as the time that I am awoken many mornings by Source to hear, listen and understand. 4:44 am is early, so I try to get to sleep as early as I can. That is my appointed time.

The fact that I sometimes choose to stay up late is apparently my issue. Even if I go to bed at 1am, if there is a conversation to be had, at 4:44 am my eyes open and I am wide awake.

And I mean wide awake. I've learned not to try to go back to sleep, but to get my pen and paper, and listen.

If I don't hear, I begin the conversation with, "Thank you God for waking me up, thank you for spending time with me and allowing us to connect in this silence." I say a prayer of gratefulness, listing what I am grateful for. Then I shut up. And listen. Then I hear.}

Many people have told me they recognize other numbers or patterns of numbers appearing to them. Some dismiss and ignore it as coincidences. What they don't realize is that signs come by the way of these situations repeating which we call "coincidences". And not just in numbers, but in events. See the coincidences. In the traditional sense, coincidences are often thought of as random acts that somehow match, resemble or support each other for no reason. This is a mis-interpretation of coincidences.

Coincidences are a mathematically precise aligning of events to provide you with signs of confirmation.

The word "coincidence" in English means two lines or shapes that lie exactly on top of each other. They appear identical. You will often see these when you pay attention. These are intentional. The Collective

Will is sharing information with you to encourage you as you move in alignment with your purposes.

Signs even come in small nudges or a strong torrent within us that some call instinct. Trust your instincts as one of the "facts" in making decisions. It will provide you with information from your heart that your head cannot and does not know.

When we are moving in the direction away from our destiny, we will see signs that may be interpreted as pain, even agony. These signs are just as important to your journey. Accept them, learn the lesson in that space so you don't repeat that mis-step again, and move in a different direction. There is no need for guilt.

Guilt is a wasted emotional ball of energy that serves no one and hurts your spirit for no reason. Guilt breeds shame and inaction. It perpetuates the lie that you are separate from the rest of us.

However, acceptance of the "wrong" choice and taking responsibility to now make a better choice breeds awareness on how to make the situation better. And if you can no longer fix the situation, it allows you a space to learn and use the experience for the good of yourself and others moving forward.

Release this habit of guilt. Self-degradation is not holy. And the pain of beating yourself up is not deserved. This is just another way of blocking the flow to your in-purpose life. These are signs that you are not moving in purpose and must make a change in order to change the outcome. You will see the signs when you pay attention. Again, these are not random occurrences. They are intentional.

Love the journey. It is all joy, so count it all joy. Be grateful for every experience and recognize how you can use it on your journey. This is difficult to remember when the experiences feel uncomfortable or painful. And you will experience these moments. We all do.

To find the presence of mind, when it feels like hell is breaking lose all around you, to be able to observe your experience and yourself, can be hard. To find a way to be grateful with understanding that what seems as evil against you will also ultimately be used for your good, can be very hard.

To find joy in that understanding, can feel impossible. But this is also power over pain. It rains on both the just and the unjust. Faith, Understanding, Gratefulness, and Joy form the umbrella. It will cover you even in tsunamis.

Even after years of living in storms, it is possible to break free. This leap of faith is one some will not find the courage within to make. They find the known pains and turmoil of their current life more comforting than the fear of stepping out into the unknown. It seems dark, lonely and scary. But the unknown is only unknown because you have not yet asked to know. Because when you ask, you will receive the answer.

When you look actively, seeking the way through the storm, on the other side of darkness, you will always find the light.

When you decide to take action in the light, knocking down inhibitions and limitations, the Universe will open up to you every good thing. Sacrificing what we are now for what we will become requires a leap into your heart and out of your head.

This change from living out of purpose to living in purpose changes our vibration. We once again become in harmony with Source. Your heartbeats fill in the missing notes, which is your purpose. And because of you, the great symphony that is the universe plays richer, more beautifully, in love, joy, happiness and peace. This music of the universe is love.

Focus on this truth, not on the storm. This is where your faith training happens. Apply faith by sowing (working deliberately for a pre-chosen outcome) the Word (your purpose spoken into you) repeatedly until it harvests (manifests through you and overflows into the world).

Hear the word spoken, which is the purpose in your heart. Accept the word by believing in your heart no matter what objections or obstacles appear. Produce a crop by taking consistent, deliberate actions until you get results.

Pray to call on God. And trust that you are heard. Then work on internalizing what you heard as your truth. None of the "secrets" that the Universe is revealing to you for success in your life will work unless you do. I understand that this may not be easy. But if we only do what is easy, our lives will be hard. If we do what is hard, with purposeful faith applied, our lives will become easy. Become good soil and sow the right seeds into your heart and your mind.

The thoughts you focus on are the seeds you are planting. In the New Age of Enlightenment, your dwelling thoughts must be carefully selected and then protected from the noise of the Information Age.

Cultivate your thoughts every day. Write down your purpose. Write it out and make it plain. The time you wake up and the time just before you go to sleep are the most vulnerable and open times to your psyche.

When you arise in the morning read your detailed vision describing your purpose out loud. Read it with energy and total belief. Use your imagination to feel and live inside of your purpose as if it is already in existence. Repeat this ritual just before you go to sleep, with the full use of your imagination.

Imagination is the fertilizer that helps your dream to grow by strengthening your heart's resolve to bring your purpose from the realm of the unseen into the world of the seen. If, during the day, you waiver or doubt, read it again. Whenever someone tells you that you can't, read it again. Whenever you seem to fail or make a mistake, read it again. Read it until it is imprinted on your heart and mind, until you believe the reality of your purpose-filled life more than the current life. Breathe your purpose rhythm every day. Dance your life.

As you enter the Age of Enlightenment, you will change. If you choose not to enter the New Age, you will still change, only without the fulfillment of who you really are. We all will feel the gain or loss of your choice, because we are One.

Humans often resist change, and that resistance is what makes change hurt. But we all do it at one time or another. But then we just have to decide to "do it hurt" until we decide not to inflict hurt on ourselves.

Everyone that does something great has to one day do what it is they are doing while "doing it hurt". But we can do it anyway. Change may feel like destruction. But greatness lives on the edge of so-called destruction. It is just restructuring. Like a phoenix rising from the ashes of what once was, you will be reborn and soar higher than you ever imagined.

There's no reason to avoid or fear change. It is always happening anyway. This current moment that you are in, change just happened. It happened again. And again.

Don't worry about a thing. Every little thing is going to be alright, and so will you. An insightful musician, Bob Marley, understood the acceptance of change and the release of worry.

Everything we do, every decision we make, sends a ripple effect of new changes throughout the world.

And their ripples flow through your life as well. Remember, we are all one. So embrace the fact that change cannot be resisted. Resisting change is like willing the sun not to rise in the morning – it's a waste of energy.

Accept the changes in the world – and in you. "Don't you worry about a thing. Cause every little thing's gonna be alright".

The paradox is that we try to protect ourselves from pain by defining borders around ourselves to show that we are singular, and therefore, unable to get hurt. The thinking is "If I don't depend on you, you can't hurt me".

The irony is, we know in our hearts that this is a lie. And all we yearn for is connection to others within our self-imposed separateness.

We live in this tension between wanting to fulfill our desire for love and connection versus the fear reaction illusion of protecting ourselves from pain that may occur within that love and connection. We must push past the borders we imposed by fear, because we have a shared identity and a shared destiny. The heartbeat of every living creature are notes combined in perfect mathematical sequence of the symphony that is the Uni-verse.

The neuro-pathways of energy which our heartbeats produce are bonds which connect us all, and this connection cannot be broken. Our brains work with our hearts to form everlasting bonds, which is the natural order of things. The chaos we are now experiencing in the world is because we have disrupted the natural order that we are One.

This chaos is also an illusion created by our delusion that we are separate from one another. The pain and turmoil seem to be escalating around the world because we are fighting against ourselves.

A house divided against itself cannot stand. The Age of Enlightenment will be when we wake up to our oneness and accept being united again. Some may be afraid of the New Age, and therefore try to stop it. But it has already begun.

Right now, it is a trickle. But it will continue until our Oneness flows and overflows, fully restoring the new world order where we all remember who we really are.

Heaven on earth is not an ideal, but a foreshadowing of what is to come. The fear driving people to stop it is not because they are bad people, but because they have simple forgotten.

They have forgotten that love and connection is the only way to stop the pain they are feeling. They are causing pain in an attempt to stop their own pain. This causes a ripple effect of more pain circling back to them.

It has been said that insanity is defined as doing the same thing repeatedly and expecting a different result. The insanity they are experiencing is because they have not yet escaped their cycle of pain. As each of us finds our way back from a life of separateness, and into oneness by living fully in our purpose, the ripples will reverse. It begins with each one of us. It begins with you.

In living our purpose, we give our highest self to the world, which is the ultimate love.

"For He so loved the world that He gave his only begotten Son…" What are you to give birth to and give to the world?

Jesus lived in His purpose, and this is the ultimate love. He was afraid at one point, but pushed through it to complete His part of the great symphony of love. Many others have also walked through fear to their purpose to bring love to the consciousness of the world – Ghandi, Mother Theresa, Muhammad, Buddah, MLK Jr., (you know of and can name others).

They all found their way into the New Age life, lighting a path for you to follow. There are many paths to climb the same mountain. As we choose our paths to express our purpose, we cross the bridge where we are fully connected into Source.

The only force of energy to ever overcome the delusion of fear is love. Love is the Truth, the Divine, the Source, the One, the God, the Creator, the I am.

This is our reality – living as who we really are in an expression of love. And we are designed to be expressions of love simply by living our true purpose of showing up as love, and contributing in love to our Oneness.

We no longer need to be constrained by the false life. Is it really living just getting through day after day, making a living, but not a true life that your heart connects with as one? It's time for a change.

Our paths are intertwined, and like the notes that form a song, we depend on each other to be counted collectively as music.

The tumult and the shouting dies;
the Captains and the Kings depart:
Still stands Thine ancient Sacrifice,
An humble and a contrite heart.
Lord God of Hosts, be with us yet,
Lest we forget – lest we forget!
                                    – Rudyard Kipling

Why have we created a separation of ourselves from our God-Source? So we can attempt to destroy the Source. Humans operate in paradoxes. We continually seek to understand and grow by disbalance. Then we attempt to reconnect through balance and harmony with the Source.

Then once we reconnect, we take our new level of understanding to again create disbalance and disharmony at this higher level. Then we repeat the cycle until we draw our body's last breath.

But this pattern does not have to be our destiny nor our mission. The climate of disharmony is our illusion of separation from our Source. In this view of separation, we can ignore God, or worship God from afar. We can look to the Divine to tell us what to do, then disobey the Instruction, and then attempt to destroy the instructor, the Source. Of course, as a result, we are attempting to destroy ourselves, because we are One.

Now we are ready as a collective One for the next level of continuous harmony – the Age of Enlightenment. In this Age, God no longer requires worship as an act of being separate. This is our time of awakening to a new level of worship and understanding. We are to worship not only with our voice, but with our actions by staying connected continuously through love of Source and love of one another.

We worship with our lives by living in our divine purpose and contributing our best selves to the Oneness of the universe.

In the famous words of Dr. Martin Luther King Jr., "I have a dream." The new churches, mosques, temples, and other houses of worship will have no more self-imposed boundaries or denominations. The walls of the factions we created as our chosen paths to worship will disappear.

As they fall away, so does our fears of one another. We will no longer point to the arm and say, you are wrong, and I, as the leg, am correct. We will no longer use our gifts of choice and of unique talents to create separation but instead, will appreciate the collective benefit.

We will no longer fear others because they appear to be different. Without fear, hate cannot exist. Without hate, we are one again free to flow in love. Love for each other, love for ourselves, and expressing that love daily by living purposely become our norm.

As more people wake up to the truth and discover the courage to make the shift into living this way, we will also discover the courage to accept and embrace a rich, full life without limitations.

Poverty illusions will fall away. "Lack" illusions will fall away. Struggle and pain, if chosen, will be used only as ways to disbalance temporarily, in order to rebalance at a higher level of understanding. Struggle and pain will no longer be a permanent state of existing because we will understand its purpose and how to properly experience it. We will use it for our lessons and enlightenment only.

Organizations of worship are made up of people. Some of these people may resist the New Age in fear of becoming obsolete. But there does not need to be fear of this shift. The people whose purpose it is to bring worship of Source and understanding to the masses are most needed in this time of the New Age.

Only the message is shifting from worship as separate from the Source into Oneness with the Source. And in this Oneness, we worship simply by expressing our pure, clean, honest, love. Such love expressed is the highest energy of Source.

Financial rewards are often one of the natural results of living a life in purposeful flow. The level of this flow of money energy depends on what we desire it to be.

The lifestyle we wish to live may be simple, uncomplicated, and without a high level of responsibility, such as employing others. We may only need a lower flow of money energy to do this, but we'll still have high levels of peace in our day to day lives, high levels of joy in our contributions to the One Source because what we desire does flow to us.

But be mindful not to look at poverty or lack and excuse these results as a "chosen" smaller financial means.

Whether you are operating in the truth of abundant flow or the lie of lack ought to be measured by your ability to manifest your purposes within the Uni-Verse with the resources available to you. Remember, there is no lack in the flow of Source. We just require varying amounts of financial flow to give our expressions of love.

Some of us desire the responsibility to help the masses to find their way back into the freedom of Oneness. This may require higher levels of money to flow through our purposeful living. Responsibility for lots of others often requires lots of money to be used in order to contribute fully in that purpose.

Neither of us is wrong or better than the other. (We are all One, after all). The amount of money made is in proportion to that which is desired to be made, and in proportion to what we wish to become, to do and to contribute to the collective whole. As we understand this better, none of us will lack for any good thing.

The ones with less financial means will still have what is needed to live in peaceful state and to express their purposeful lives. The ones with more financial energy flow will understand how to use this to express their purposes, in ways that ensure the Oneness is nourished and cared for.

The contributions financially will not be made in burdened charity to the cruel, lazy and undisciplined (the unenlightened), but through loving expression of our gifts and talents. We will ensure that the basic needs of food, shelter, education and safety are available for all. This is not under a label of socialism, communism, or any other label, but as an expression of overflowing abundance and love.

In this environment, the education of the masses will be with the purpose to share the message of the New Age. This message of purposeful living, when received by those in need, will allow them the insight to lead themselves out of the illusion of lack (of money, of love, of peace, etc), out of the illusion of poverty, war, fear, hate, and division, and to transcend the pain and hurt they are experiencing, when they are ready to embody the One Law.

Some of us who have already obtained great financial wealth may still be in need of release from a separateness mindset. In other words, the presence or absence of great monetary wealth alone is not an indicator of living a purposeful, loving life.

A life of chosen smaller financial means is no more proof of purposeful living than a life of chosen wealth. A life of chosen wealth is no more proof of purposeful living than a life of chosen smaller financial means. This had to be written both ways for clarity's sake. A belief in using this benchmark of righteousness is just another way of creating an illusion of separation.

Humans are the only creatures who set a trap, then willingly step into the cage. We must be aware of this financial measurement trap to avoid setting it for ourselves.

How long do we have to transition into our purposeful living? In our perceived individualism, no one knows. As a collective One, we have until we do it. Time is not a measurement of what is. The Age of Enlightenment already was, and is, and will come again. It is only our awareness of its existence that is shifting.

Motivational speaker Jim Rohn once asked why there were people in the Bible who lived hundreds of years, but we no longer seem to have that option. It occurred to me that we may, as a collective whole, have decided to shorten our bodily existence on earth. There may be a number of reasons why but I can only surmise. Perhaps we realized that we are no longer living connected as one to each other or the Source of us all. In our disconnect, the result might be the destruction of our world and of ourselves. As a way to slow down this pattern of downward spiral, we may have decided to terminate us as individuals at a much more rapid rate.

Imagine if a destructive, egoistic person had 800 years to live rather than 80 years! We may have figured out that if the egoistic individual dies in body, it might make room for another being that would stay connected and light the way for others to follow. This may have been how humans decided to move from the individual ego-driven self, back into the Oneness of the Creator.

Because we all know at a spiritual level that we are One, perhaps we have decided to speed up the process of spirits learning life lessons with shorter individual lives, so we can rebalance and connect in our next life experience. The ultimate result would be the enlightenment of us all with purposeful living and a clear understanding that there is only One of us.

But now we are awakening. We are remembering. So we are living longer. We will once again be able to live hundreds of years if necessary, to fulfill our purposes.

We use pronouns to describe our One Source – He, She, God, Goddess, and many other terms. The One is not limited by the forms of these descriptions. We are all created in God's image. Therefore, God is both male and female, as we in our limited understanding have perceived it, and so much more.

We are all created in God's image; therefore, God is all of us. Therefore, we are all of God. We, you and I, are one. We are one breath, one cosmic heartbeat. We are the I Am.

The I Am is Spirit, a fluid, uncontainable, unlimited, abundant, whole being. As soon as we, humans, recognize, realize, accept, and acknowledge that this is also the description of the collective us, we will set ourselves free from the self-imposed cages we placed ourselves in.

When people understand the true nature of the power behind Ghandi, Jesus, Mother Theresa, Martin Luther King, Jr., and the like, they will no longer feel the need to jump on the "anti-..." movements. The realization that fighting against what we don't want is exactly what perpetrates its existence is the key to spectacular freedom from it. When we focus on what we do not want, we feed the beast what it craves most, our energetic attention. And in so doing, we bond ourselves to it, both individually and in our collective oneness of the universal One.

Instead, whenever humans have figured out to focus on what good we desire, we have been rewarded with spectacular results. Instead of focusing on ways to stop hatred, focus on all the ways to expand love. This is the universal law of expansion, properly applied.

All things, when fed our energic attention, expand. All things, whether categorized as "good" or "evil", have the inherent desire for expansion and growth. All things, whether living or non, are made up of energy. And when one adds energy to energy, energy expands exponentially. Step one is understanding this universal law.

Step two is applying this universal law consistently. As we, as the collective One, begin to experience more and more individuals feeding energy into love, abundance, peace, togetherness, supportiveness, and gratefulness, we will finally fully realize who we are. We are the One. We are creators of our own lives. We are creators of our world. We are creators of our universe. We are creators of our multiverse. We are both the artists and the canvas. Our words and actions are the paint brushes. Our focused energy is the paint.

What color energy are you choosing? What kind of word and action brushes are you using? Do you have a positive plan for your precious canvas, or are you just allowing anyone and anything to fall upon it? Are you training yourself, dear artist, in the proper techniques to manifest in the art of expansion? The chapters that follow in this book are to help with your artistic training of yourself.

This is not easy, I know. It takes effort to shift from the way we have always done things. Mental and emotional and physical energy must all be summoned and like a laser, focused on the love we are. This is not easy while there are still "individuals" misusing and misunderstanding the law of expansion. These misuses expand the experiences of pain, despair, lack, and all the other lies we have created. To focus on love in the face of that, is not easy.

But it is possible. Ghandi proved that. Nelson Mandela proved that. And now, you shall prove that as well. If we are to experience our Universal Oneness, it is necessary. The individuals are waking up from the slumber. We are Becoming. The secrets of the universal Oneness that we are, are no longer secrets to whosoever chooses to learn them. You are ready. Study. Learn. Apply the One Law.

Repeat until successful. Then repeat until it becomes once again your nature. Yes, this was once your nature to operate only in love and abundance. But you forgot who you are. We all did. Now you are remembering. That small stirring deep inside your chest, that swirling in your abdomen, the pulsating through your body – you are remembering the truth. Through that truth, your abundance flows.

You, powerful One. I, powerful One. We, Powerful One.

Humanity is remembering who we were in the "Garden of Eden", the time of full flowing abundance. And we are moving once again to living as our real self. The result must be the Garden. In this space, which will cover the earth, there is only the truth of abundance, never lack.

In this space, technology will have had evolved to the point where people are only using their time to pursue the cultivation of their mind, body and souls. In doing so, they are bringing their best forth. Their best adds to the One Mind, expanding the multiverse. The Garden is already here, waiting for us to rediscover her.

Heaven, paradise, Garden of Eden, enlightenment, and many other names found throughout most religions and referred to throughout history – these are all names for the same. You see, on some level, we remember.

But our current experiment of living out of alignment with our highest selves has overshadowed our memories of perfection. "Perfection" is not the definition we now use. Perfection is about being in full alignment with love. This alignment always results in peace, joy, truth and abundance.

The pain done to your heart in your past human experience can now be released. You no longer need to hold on to it in order to exercise the illusion that you can protect yourself in the future. First, the pain you experienced was experienced by the spirit being in you, as fertilizer, in order to help you to grow into the beautiful soul that you are, able to nourish others with your experience. So do not instead continue to poison yourself by holding onto the fertilizer. It did its job. Now it is time to do yours.

Trying to protect oneself from future pain by holding onto the memories of the past pain is an exercise in futility because there is no past and no future. There is only the present. And in the present moment, you are exactly where you need to be to experience what you need to experience, whether characterized as "good" or "bad", so that you can continue to grow, and then one day fully remember the collective One that you are.

The pain done to your heart can be healed, can be released with forgiveness of yourself and forgiveness of the unenlightened soul that perpetrated the hurt that you experienced. Whether small hurts, or big "unforgivable" hurts, it is time to release them all.

If you are still in the midst of experiencing your pain, trust that it will end. Then look for ways to move away from the perpetrator of the pain. Seek help and keep going this until you get it. You are not alone. Your pain is our pain and we want you to be free. You do not deserve to suffer, and it is no one's right to make you suffer. Even while in the midst of their unenlightened actions, Ghandi, Mandela, Jesus, Mother Theresa forgave their "oppressors". They understood the power of forgiveness.

Instead, be for love. Be for peace. Be for-give. Give yourself the gift of forgiveness, fully, completely, freely, and without reservation. Be grateful for the lesson that helped you to grow, release the teacher from the bondage you have held yourself to with unforgiveness, and move forward.

Forgiveness is the greatest gift you can give to yourself. Forgive them. Forgive yourself. And do better now. Use the methods in the following chapters to bring to light the most amazing versions of who you are. It is time.

You are not damaged or broken, unless you choose to continue to hold onto the fertilizer of past pain. There is no longer any need for it. It has done its job. Now, do yours. Be grateful for the lesson that you can choose to use to grow.

There's a saying - knowledge is power. Whoever said that got it wrong. I "know" a lot of stuff that I have not used, and it gave me no power whatsoever. But if we expand the definition of knowing to include application, only then is the power possible. In clearer words - Do Something With What You Know. And you know a lot already. The rest, you will acquire along your journey to applying the One Law to your life.

In the subsequent chapters, there are several short sections. Do not let the brevity fool you - when you do as suggested in each section, you will have an understanding of yourself like never before. You'll more clearly identify your values, who and what really matters to you, your chosen purposes for your life. You'll also expand your current knowledge so you'll have even more resources to use as you continue to show yourself and the world who you really are.

Some of the sections can be done quickly. Others may take more time. Just go step by step beginning with number 1 until you are done. Don't feel overwhelmed. You only need to focus on one item at a time. When you complete it, pause, reflect, and CELEBRATE!!! Lock into your nervous system that you have just done something that most people in the world never do - think about how you want to really live your life.

By reading this book, you are in the elite 10%. By applying the guidance, you are in the outstanding 1%. Step by step, and when you look back at the end, you will clearly see the One Law fully operational in your life. So, get excited - and get started!

Remember, when you decide to take action in the light, knocking down inhibitions and limitations, the Universe will open up to you every good thing.

Sacrificing what we are now for what we will become requires a leap into your heart and out of your head.

CHAPTER 1 : Higher Habits - How to Create the Foundation for YOU

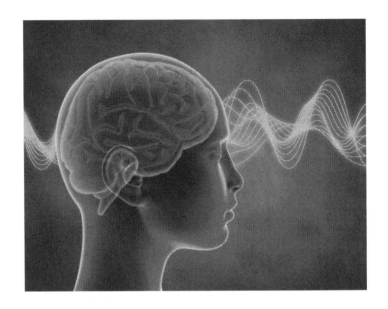

1. **Emerge!**

Create the person you want to be by releasing the person you really are.

Emergence of the REAL YOU, your highest, loving powerful self is the recipe for true success in life. Throughout this book, you will be the artist. You will actively decide what is on your canvas of life. You will select the colors and the brush to make it possible. You will empower yourself with the skills to use these powers within you in the right ways to create a beautiful amazing, truly abundant life.

Without negative judgement, look at your life as it really is. Did you decide how you are currently living? Did you choose your career? Are you feeling fulfilled and that you are contributing in a good way with what you are doing? How are you financially? Are you feeling shortage and lack or do you have enough to live, grow and contribute as much as your heart desires? Examine your health. Are you full of energy and vitality? If not, why not? How are your relationships with your intimate partner? With your family and friends? Are they full of love and connection? Let's explore the possibilities for the REAL YOU, the healthy, happy, whole you that is living a deliberate, purposeful life. It's time to allow yourself to dream again. Because it's now time to create your dream.

2. Create Good Habits!

Select a special book (a journal, a big sketchbook, or a digital medium that you can easily access) to gather the information as you Create Good Habits.

Throughout this book, what you'll create will directly and immediately begin to bring to light what matters most to your heart. You will answer the age-old question of "Why am I here?" "What's my purpose(s)?" "Where did I come from?" "Where am I going?" Record your answers and "remembering moments" each day as you do the following exercises. A life worth living is a life worth recording. So pick that special book that speaks to you.

You may prefer to do it digitally, but I highly recommend going "old school" on this. There is something magical that happens when you put pen to paper between your brain, heart and hand. But if you insist on digital, it's better than not doing it at all.

I do love that my journals are the most valuable books in my home library to me. I rarely re-read items I've written saved in folders on my computer or in the cloud. But my hand-written journals are a constant source of reference, reminder, and reflection.

3. Write Your Destiny Letter!

This is YOUR CONTRACT FOR SUCCESS! Right now, right here, write out your future.

Ask yourself "What would it look like if I were the man or woman I want to be? What if there were no limits, no boundaries, nothing out of my reach?" Allow yourself to daydream, feel this excitement and get prepared to capture it in writing RIGHT NOW!

The best version of you, the "you" of the future, can begin to live now. Write a letter to your present self from your future self. By capturing the life you dream of in specific words and clear images, you breathe life into this amazing being. This is the recipe for your life success. So, take time for yourself with this step.

I took a week by myself, away from work, family and friends, and daily obligations. In a small cabin in the middle of nowhere, I got quiet and still. I listened to the voice in my soul and captured the whisperings of my heart on paper. Yes, go old school and use paper and pen to engage your heart - do not type this, which often engages your head.

Allow your imagination to flow freely. Go 10 years into the future. Tell the you of today who you have become once you finally opened your heart fully and really lived full out. You released fear of judgement from others, and from yourself. You accepted the truth that you are enough, that you are worthy, and that you are good enough. You opened your heart to the reality that you deserve the best life has to offer. You relinquished ownership of past mistakes. You threw away your right to be hurt, angry, and betrayed.

You instead chose to forgive all and see everyone as blameless, freeing yourself of those weights. You look at yourself with total love and acceptance, using only encouraging words. You embrace your beautiful, uniqueness and hold it up for all the world to behold and admire. You finally live as the real you, the best version of yourself, not as an imitation of others nor as an idea of who other people decided you should be.

You are safe. You are free. You have finally fully emerged and there are no limits here. From this place within, tap into who you have become as a result of living this way.

Capture the details of who you have become.
How and where are you living?
What matters most to you and how does it show in your life?
Who are you able to help?
How are you bettering the world?
What benefits do you bring to your family?
What does life feel like for you and your family?
What kinds of friends do you have and what do you do together?
What does it feel like in your strong, fit body?
With your abundance of energy, flexibility, memory, and confidence in your physical self, what adventures are you having?
How do you show gratefulness each day?
What do you do for your spiritual fulfillment?
What does a day in your life look like?
What are your morning rituals?
How are you having fun?

Remember, there are no limits in this future. What is your financial picture?

How is money flowing through you?

What charities are you helping from your overflow?

Allow the future you to express how grateful you feel to your present self for opening your heart, trusting in yourself and for believing that everything you need will appear as you need it.

Feel what it is like to be the real, limitless, beautiful, healthy, loved, free and complete YOU. Capture those feeling in words, with more and more details. Smile as you write. Laugh out loud in sheer joy. Breathe it in deeply, and with each release of breath, know that it is all real.

In doing this exercise, the real you of the future has connected with the you of today, in love and openness, and shown you the truth. Now that you have written your letter, this will serve as your contract with the Universe. Your options for abundant, overflowing experiences are now reconnected with you today. Get ready to experience this amazing life.

4. I Am Yourself

A name is not just something you tell people to call you. A name is a definition of what you see inside the package. Every time your name is spoken, with it are spoken your dreams and aspirations, your hopes and your desires. Our names are arguably the most important word to us. So take some time to explore your present name. What are the meanings of your given names? Look it up. I created a poem of my given name using the various meanings and historical references I found. In this poem, I honor my name and see that "I Am" the beauty it represents.

5. Name Your Future Self

What do you feel when you think about what your name is saying about who you really are? If your highest version of you doesn't resonate with it – change it. We are no longer children. Decide what empowering name you want to be called, and add it to the list of names you use. You can select a different version of your name or nickname as I have, or an entirely different name.

How do the memories you attach to your present name measure up to the Future You detailed in your Destiny Letter? What name would you call the future you by that could capture his or her spirit? As you go through this journey of transformation and emerging as your highest self, you may find yourself slipping into old habits and patterns.

A quick way to remind yourself of the new you is to call her or his name. Just as someone calling your name gets your attention, calling the name of your Highest Self brings your attention back to the real you. Say this name. Call yourself this name aloud. How does that feel? Weird? Empowering? Hopeful? Throughout each day, enjoy the flavor of your Future Self name in your mouth. Become one with this name more and more each day by doing the suggestions throughout this book.

6. Lean into the dream!
- Pull out your Destiny Letter, your universal contract, and read it line by line.

- Divide each thing into manageable baby action steps. Begin with this year then increase until you reach year 10. For example, if you want to be an artist who painted 30 paintings, set baby steps to paint 2 paintings in year one, 2 paintings in year two, 2 paintings in year three, 3 paintings in year four, 3 paintings in year five, 3 paintings in year six, 3 paintings in year seven, 3 paintings in year eight, 4 paintings in year nine and 5 paintings in year ten. You have now completed your minimum of 30 paintings. The momentum of experiencing success and consistency will likely propel you to complete many more. But you get the idea.

- Focus only on the actions this year for now. Put all of your energy into becoming the person who can complete this action. Practice. Learn and do the things that (Insert your Power Name here) would do to get this result. Celebrate your "2 paintings" completed for year one.

- Next year, focus on next year's action steps.

7. Write Your Eulogy

If today was your last day on earth, what would the people that know you best say about you? Be honest with the good and the not so good stuff.

Guess what? It's not too late. You can improve starting right now, right where you are. Compare your eulogy of today with your Destiny Letter from your future self.

- write down where the gaps are

-   start planning how to shift your daily decisions to reduce the gap between who you are now and who you have determined that you are destined to be.

8. Set Your Intentions

At the beginning of each week, get clear on exactly what you want to become, do and have for the upcoming week that supports your highest self. Write down the important things which you must do in order to be and have what your heart desires. This is not a to-do list. This is a decision capture of the outcomes that really matter to you.

-   Pick 1 (ONE!!!) thing per day that will move you closer to your destiny and work on completing a specific part of that.

Writing down your 1 thing anchors it as most important for your day, so when the noise of the world kicks in, it doesn't drown out the music of your soul's desire.

9. Check In with Yourself

The major key to your better future is YOU, so take time to check in with yourself. Ask some key questions:

"How am I defining success?"

"Is this really my definition of success, or is it one that I have inherited, learned or accepted from others?"

"What did I do today to make this day successful, for my heart's desires?"

"Who am I being right now? Does this help make my life successful?"

Reflect on the answers. Write down your answers in your journal to see the patterns so you can identify where to make the 2mm micro-adjustments towards hitting your target.

CHAPTER 2 : Higher Heart - How to Connect with the Inner YOU

SPIRIT

10. Spirit self, are you asking life affirming questions or are you asking questions that kill your spirit and hope?

Are you looking, with expectation and emotion, for the good things, or are you focusing on finding faults and failures?

Are you sitting still, watching your dreams die or are you taking action steps – small daily steps – in the direction of your dreams?

Ask, and it will be given you, seek, and you will find; knock, and the door will be opened to you. For everyone who asks receives; the one who seeks, finds; and the one who knocks, the door will be opened. – Matthew 7:7-12 (NIV)

"For I know the plans I have for you", declares the Lord, "plans to prosper you and not to harm you, plans to give you hope and a future". – Jeremiah 29:11 (NIV)

Included in the YOU Plans are:

- Plans to Prosper You: This means abundance in every area of your life is within you

-        Plans to Give You Hope: This means the right words, the power to love and to forgive and to keep going are all within you.

-        Plans to Give You a Future: This means you have a purpose for existing and a destiny to fulfill. You are special and the world needs you.

The designer of YOU has the blueprints used to make you and knows who you are and what you are capable of doing. Now go out and build on that.

Prayer: I pronounce blessing over limitations, releasing the anointing of God over things, situations, and persons, which releases the potential within, giving blessing the opportunity to manifest divinely. I believe that blessings reverse and prevent curses, breaking all negative cycles, turning situations into multiple streams of prosperity.

Prayer is about focusing on the truth of who you are, and whose you are. You are a child of the Creator, the "I AM". Because of this, any words you speak following the words "I am…" are creating, as well. Do this deliberately. Which words will you use to emerge the YOU that you really are?

A version of St. Francis' Prayer:
Lord, make me an instrument of thy peace.

Where there is hatred, let me sow love'
where injury, pardon;
where doubt, faith;
where despair, hope;
where darkness, light;
where sadness, joy;
Oh Divine Master, grant that I may not so much seek
to be consoled, as to console;
to be understood, as to understand;
to be loved, as to love.
For it is in giving that we receive;
in pardoning that we are pardoned;
in dying to self that we are born to eternal life.

Based on what you believe, select prayers or affirmations that you can use to fill up that special place deep inside of yourself every morning, and whenever you need a charge from the events of life.

GRATEFULNESS

11. Connect yourself regularly with the high frequency emotions:

Love
Gratitude
Joy
Passion
Satisfaction

Happiness

Excitement

Joyful expectation

Hope

Peacefulness

12. Each morning, read your Destiny Letter (number 3), then say out loud: "I am grateful for this and something better. I trust. I am open. I am ready. I am that I am sends me."

13. Wake Up in Gratefulness.

Each day when you open your eyes, say "Thank you". The fact that you have woken up is proof that you still have value to add to the world, you still have love to give and that you are loved. Each morning is a chance to reset your life onto a more empowering path of light, love and laughter. Saying "thank you" is acknowledging the gift of today.

Acknowledging the gift of today keeps you more present and focused on taking deliberate, now-actions rather than slipping back into the mediocre habits of yesterday. Today, you have another chance to be the best version of you! So, open your heart to receive your gift, feel the specialness of it, and say earnestly, "thank you".

FAMILY TIME

14. Having people to love and be loved be loved is the ultimate success. Take time to listen to your loved ones. Listen to what's being said, and even more crucial, what's not being said.

Tony Robbins said "Every communication is either a loving communication or a cry for help." If you are not feeling love from your family in what they are saying to you, then open your heart to listen to what they really need from you.

Are they scared? Lonely? Confused? Hurt? Do they just need you to be quiet and listen openly and without judgement? A wonderful way to show them love is to be present and be quiet. Take time to listen to them.

15. Making quality time consistently to be with your family and friends matters. What was the last quality thing you did with the people that you love?
Quality + Quantity = Showing Love

16. Would you like the magic keys to unlock the gates between those you love and yourself?

These simple words, when directed to the source of your pain, can transform the experience in a moment:

"I am sorry."

"Please forgive me."

"I love you."

"Thank you."

(Dr. Hew Len)

Practice saying these words in every situation that needs to be made better. Practice reciting these words inside of yourself every day. The shift is remarkable.

Use these words deliberately, and with an open heart to transform pain into passion. Tell your ego to "SHUT UP!" Your ego won't keep you warm at night, won't hold you when you cry, and won't celebrate the good moments with you. And your ego will never sit by your bed, holding your hand near the end of this life.

But, if you show consistently that you love your family, they will be there.

17. Your intimate relationship matters, so treat it like it matters. GO ALL IN on your love relationship. Intentionally spend time together by setting and scheduling connection rituals. Scheduling love may seem cold or mechanical, but it's just the opposite. This is an act of declaration that the relationship with your partner is priority over the day to day issues and responsibilities. Some ideas:

-       Daily ritual of 30-60 minutes together, just talking and sharing about your day. Go for a walk, sit in the garden, or any place that it will be one-on-one focus and alone time.

-       Weekly ritual of a quiet night alone for romance, sex and connection - pick a set night each week. This is to ensure that the minimum attention is given to this important area consistently. If you feel so moved on other nights during the week, go for it as well!

-       Quarterly and/or yearly rituals: Depending on your financial situation, plan to get away 1 - 4 times per year for one week together (no kids, no friends, no family, no work). Spend the time to go deep in getting to know each other (we all continue to change and grow), to share life visions and values, and to just have fun exploring the world together.

MEDITATION

18. Worry is a form of negative meditation. It is a habit of having imaginary conversations with yourself or other people in imaginary situations that will likely never happen. Unfortunately, this habit causes the same pain, anxiety, doubts, anger and fear as if the event actually took place. Instead of engaging in negative meditation, ask yourself just 4 questions from Dale Carnegie to shift into positive meditation and action:

1.   What am I worried about?

2.   Can I do anything about it – if "No", then there is no need to worry. Just let it go. – if "Yes", go to step three.

3.   Here's what I'm going to do about it. Write out your plan of action.

4.   When am I going to start doing it?

19. Whatever you focus on expands. If you focus on what you want, it will increase in an endless bounty of blessings. If you focus on what you don't want, it will multiply in your life like gremlins in water. Control your thoughts to control your focus.

When faced with an event, a thought will occur about what you feel it means. If the thought triggers disempowering emotions, ask yourself "What else could this event mean?" Then deliberately choose a thought that causes you to feel empowered.

Practice now. Write down something that happened that you did not like from your past. Notice the emotions that still may be present from this time that no longer exists. These emotions are an indication of the meanings you have attached to this event. To free yourself from unempowering emotions that you may still be carrying, simply change the meanings you give to this event. With a new choice of meaning, comes new emotions.

Keep changing the meanings until you connect with loving, freeing, grateful, understanding, or any other uplifting emotions. This is how your re-focus can free you from your past. Repeat this process every time you are caught in disempowering emotions. This could be applied to memories, to current experiences, and to when we're thinking about what may happen in the future.

20. I suggest learning Benjamin Franklin's Magic Formula Checklist for Success. These 13 virtues, when improved upon regularly will help you become the person you need to become in order to have the life you detailed in your Destiny Letter (number 3).

How do you honestly feel you rank on a scale of 1 (lowest) to 5 (highest) in each area? Is there something you can do today to improve in any area? Take action NOW to improve in areas you can, and celebrate NOW in the areas that you are crushing it in!

- Temperance
- Silence
- Order
- Resolution
- Frugality

- Industry
- Sincerity
- Justice
- Moderation
- Cleanliness
- Tranquility
- Chastity
- Humility

Write a few words as your definition/explanation for each word to explain how you will embody the virtues.

21. Time to get your kindergarten spirit on! It's Vision Board time!

- Grab some glue or tape, scissors, and every old magazine you can get your hands on.
- Sit on the floor or on the grass (grounding yourself to the earth).
- Go page by page. Cut out every picture, phrase or words that attract your attention. You can also print pictures, phrases and words off the internet.
- Create a collage with some of your finds that inspires you, symbolizes the life you'd like to experience, and speaks to your soul.
- Put it up in your home where you can see it daily.

Be amazed as you watch your Vision Board come to life just for you! Meditating on your future in picture form is a powerful mechanism to being a deliberate creator.

22. What is your power symbol? Decide on a representation of your highest self, your boldest aspiration, your drive to continue on in the face of danger, your inspiration and hopefulness. Keep your symbol visible in your environment.

For example, my symbols are the tiger, for its strength, beauty, focus, and gracefulness; and the butterfly for its transformational qualities, courage to fly, and limitless travel. I also have selected a flower, number, stone, bird and color. So I have created many ways to tap into my power.

Look for inspiration and ideas in your favorite Flowers, Animals, Color, Precious Stone, Insects, Birds, and Numbers.

FORGIVENESS

23. Forgiveness is one of the most misunderstood words in the human experience. First, let's consider what forgiveness is NOT.

It is not condoning or accepting bad behavior. It is not giving permission for the act to continue or to happen again. It is not giving power to the person that you are forgiving. It is not a way to ensure it doesn't happen again. And it is not only available after some time or penance has been paid.

So, what is forgiveness? It is a decision to take the next step of your life without carrying the useless weights of past events. The betrayals, the hurts, the pains, the let-downs, the kicks, bumps and bruises - those done to us, and those we've inflicted, all deserve to be forgiven. Why? Because the past cannot be changed, but it can be redefined.

Instead of being angry at the boss that fired you, can you see the more fulfilling job you found afterwards as a gift from that boss? Instead of wallowing in the pain your ex caused, can you remember the good moments shared and see how the challenges were your tools to know what you really want in a partner and how to be a better person in your next relationship?

Instead of beating yourself up over what you did to yourself or to someone else, can you accept it as a choice of your past, and now you have the ability to be and do better now? You can move forward to an abundance of love in the space of forgiveness.

Who in your life do you need to forgive? It's not for them - it's for you. Write their names down in your journal in the sentence <u>"(Name), I forgive you. I release the poison of blame and reclaim my power."</u> Do this for each person you need to forgive.

And now also put your own name in the sentence, and forgive yourself. Yes, you do deserve to be forgiven. It's time to let the past go, so you can become the best version of you today. The world needs you to forgive yourself and grow. Say the sentences out loud. Again.

I sometimes have to repeat this exercise over and over again until I fully release the pain. But it is worth it to feel that loving flow of peace again.

CHAPTER 3 : HIGHER HEAD – Training your Mind and Using Your Imagination Intentionally

24 – 29 Read

30 – 34 Journal

35 – 39 Motivational

READ

24. Recommend reading or listening to the recording on YouTube "How to Stop Worrying and Start Living" by Dale Carnegie.

Yes, it's over 9 hours. But break it up into bite size pieces. Listen for 30-60 minutes a day until complete. This amazing recording will change your life! Invest the time in yourself. Release worry from your routine. You are worth it.

I listen to this recording at least once a year to remind myself of the simple but important message - stop worrying and start doing.

25. Recommend learning the 10 Laws of Success in the book <u>The Greatest Salesman in the World</u> by Og Mandino.

I put each one on a card and taped them around my mirror to remind me to live a higher life.

26. Recommend reading <u>The Richest Man in Babylon</u> by George S. Clason to help you to secure your financial fortune with easy to understand lessons in story form. Be transported to far away lands.

27. Create a vehicle to live in that is your body, mind, and spirit as a strong trifecta. Learn how by answering the questions in the book <u>Fork Disease! Go Vegan!</u> Order your hardcopy or ebook today on Amazon. Yes, I wrote it, so I know it can really make a difference in how you take care of yourself. Your body is the only one you'll get, so take care of it.

28. Recommend reading The God Memorandum in The Greatest Miracle in the World by Og Mandino, pages 353-367.

Accept the challenge posed to the main character by reading this manifesto. For the next 100 days, take just 10 minutes to remember who you really are.

29. Recommend doing the exercise in chapter 3 of Money Master the Game by Tony Robbins to figure out the REAL numbers you require to be financially secure, financially independent, and financially free. Learn the true amount of money to make your dreams a winnable game. You may be much closer than you imagine…

Money is a necessary tool in order to live life on your terms. He shows how to take the steps necessary to create:

1.   Financial Security where your basic needs of are covered with your job income.
2.   Financial Independence where no job is needed and your basic needs are still covered
3.   Financial Freedom when EVERYTHING YOU CAN THINK OF is covered and your money is working for you!

The surprise is that the actual monetary amount to experience life at each level is probably A LOT less than you think!

JOURNAL

30. Be encouraged every day. Listen to, read, and watch things daily to fill you up with words of hope and courage. You'll need this to make withdrawals from when life gets tough. This includes the resource you are creating with your journal. Read what you are writing in your journals when you need encouragement. This is you reminding yourself of what really matters, of the power you possess, and of the vision you hold.

Look back through the pages now and marvel at how much you have already transformed into an even more amazing you.

31. Our brains are designed to generate ideas, and to grow them. It is not made to be a storage facility.

Use your journal to capture the ideas that come to you. These seeds just become the foundation of your transformation. Have an idea? Write it down quickly! Idea... Try... Do... Do Again... And Again... Keep Doing... Success!

32. How do you reach your goal? By tapping into the goldmine between your ears. Grab your journal. Right now, dedicate just 60 minutes to exercise your mind. Put your goal at the top of the paper. Do not censor yourself or edit your ideas.

Write at least 20 ideas on how you can improve yourself, your skills, your environment, your associations, and your service to others in ways that will help you reach your goal. Do this exercise for any goal that you have. You'll be amazed at what you intuitively already know.

33. Once a year, take time off for a full week, or for a full month, if you are able. Be alone. Be still. Be open. Ideas and insights flow freely through us from the Universe when we listen. Use your mental gold mind to bring your golden life into reality. Calendar this time right now. Lock it in. Commit to your alone time to reflect and connect with yourself.

34. Say "I think deliberately and with a purpose every day." Use the goldmine between your ears at a special time each day.

Create the life you want to live by capturing your ideas and magic moments. Make thinking a deliberate part of your day. Calendar 30-60 minutes for yourself daily to be still and connect.

Recommendation: Add this thinking time and journaling to your morning rituals. You are fresh-minded and most connected to your subconscious first thing in the morning. Write down your ideas no matter how far-fetched or silly you may think it is. In time, you may see what you cannot now understand. Just capture it in writing so when that time comes, you can remember what gold you have unearthed.

MOTIVATIONAL

35. Do you know that you are a superhero? You have been endowed with 10 powers. When used intentionally, for your good, you can do miraculous feats that will amaze the world! You have the power to:

think
love
will
laugh
imagine
create
plan
speak
pray

and most importantly, the power to choose!

(Source: The Greatest Miracle in the World by Og Mandino)

Take this moment to reflect on your superhero powers. Play with time. Practice them. Pull them out every day, you amazing superhero!

36. Commit to your disciplines. This is not a bad word when applied correctly. Discipline is about deciding beforehand what really matters to you that will contribute to the emerging of your highest self, and choosing not to let the many other options interfere with your doing those things.

Jim Rohn said "Discipline feels better than regret. Someday is today, so get to work! Do today what others won't do, so you can then have tomorrow what others don't have. Discipline yourself to walk the "straight and narrow road" of empowering choices over worthless whims. Defend your most cherished desires from your most casual wishes. As a result, you will become who you want to be, and live how you really want to live."

So my friend, what really matters that will change the trajectory of your life? Will you commit to doing it for the next 24 hours? Tomorrow you can do another 24 hours of good choices. In the words of songstress Dinah Washington, "what a difference a day makes… 24 little hours...brought the sun and the flowers, where there used to be rain".

37. Read, learn, grow, hustle, repeat. What you are doing today to feed your highest self is not a temporary situation. Just like we must eat throughout our lives in order to live, we must also continue the upward process of growth if we are to reach our destiny. The Universe desires you to have everything you want. Do you have the same desire? How does it show in what you do each day? Write your answers in your journal.

38. The power to choose is our greatest power. We are always using this power. The only question is "are we choosing - intentionally or by default?" Here's a wonderful list of choices that Og Mandino offered in his book "The Greatest Miracle in the World".

Choose to love...rather than hate.
laugh...cry
create...destroy
persevere...quit
praise...gossip
heal...wound
give...steal

act...procrastinate

grow...not

pray...curse

live...die

Choose wisely because it will dictate who you become. Who you become will decide what kind of life you get to live and how much of your power you can tap into.

39. Ask yourself motivational questions.

Language matters - a lot! How we ask ourselves a question is just as important as the question itself. Want to motivate yourself to take empowered actions? Ask empowering questions. What you focus on expands, so ask questions that help you to focus on finding your path to amazing.

Examples:

Who am I being and who am I becoming to make my life more successful?

How can I improve the results I've achieved?

CHAPTER 4: HIGHER HARVEST – Enjoy the Benefits of Being Your Best Self

MONEY

40. Paying yourself first is not just a nice theory. It's a necessity to break the cycle of debt and lack. It creates an awareness in your spirit that you matter, that there is only abundance, and that you are in control of your money, not the world.

Save 10% of everything that comes through your hands in an emergency fund until you have at least 6 months of income saved. Then continue your habit by wisely investing that same percentage.

This may seem like a hard thing to do if you are barely getting by now. But if you want to experience something different, you'll have to do something different. Even if you can't do 10%, do 5%, or 3%. Just commit to a percentage and do it consistently.

When you have an emergency fund, you'll stop having a financial crisis with your life crisis. Life crisis will happen. Financial crisis doesn't have to. Automate this transfer of funds into a separate, secure account.

41. Gambling is a foolish "investment". Don't be misled by get rich quick or easy money "opportunities".

Where are you gambling away your seed money? Instead learn legitimate ways to invest. Educate yourself. If you can't seem to help yourself from going after the high of the next "sure thing", give yourself the gift of Gambler's Anonymous or other support groups.

42. Invest where your principal (money invested) is safe, where it can be reclaimed if needed, and where you'll get a fair interest rate above the inflation rate.

If you invest in riskier investments where the principle is at risk, be sure that if you lose the investment, you don't cause suffering and pain. How? By making a balanced portfolio. Don't put all your eggs in one basket because even if you don't drop the basket, someone may kick it over.

Before investing, consulting with wise people experienced (and trustworthy) in the profitable handling of money. Check out the book <u>Unshakeable</u> by Tony Robbins to ensure you don't get taken by what some financial "experts" try to do.

Adopt the philosophy of the wise investor: reduce risks while maximizing returns.

43. Before making a loan, assure their ability to repay and their reputation for doing so. Don't be too confident in your own wisdom over the reality of the borrower.

If the banks consider someone a poor investment risk, stop to consider why. If you lend to family, there is a likelihood that you will not be repaid. Destroying family bonds over money is the most foolish investment move of all. So, if you choose to lend to family, consider making it a gift or a joint venture. Otherwise, just say no.

44. Numbers matter. And not just the number of candles on your birthday cake! Know your financial numbers, even if you are afraid to look. This is where you regain control of your money, your business, and most importantly, your life.

Questions to Answer For Your Truth Now and to Create Your Future:

- How much money do you now have access to? (not credit, actual cash)
- How much money do you owe? (look at everything owed to everyone and add it all up)
- How much money do you have coming in this month? Next month? (look at all sources of income, not just your job)
- What money do I have invested? How are my investments structured?

Now you know your present reality. From here, you can make changes to your behaviors and create plans for a more prosperous future.

FUTURE SELF

45. Often we forget our most precious commodity - time. Time is the one thing we all must learn to use with respect. I believe that we are born not knowing our appointed end because the "not knowing" creates an urgency to live our lives.

We ought to take action to reveal the person we are designed to be. There ought to be an urgency to doing what we are destined to do now, because tomorrow is not promised.

People tend to look at the years passed, but fail to recognize the moments that made it happen. I came across a poem that reminds me to choose wisely how I spend every moment.

"I've only just a minute, only 60 seconds in.
It was forced upon me, I can't refuse it,
I didn't seek it, and I didn't choose it -
but it's up to me to use it.
I must suffer if I lose it; Give account if I abuse it;
It's only a tiny little minute - but eternity is in it.

-Author unknown

How are you treasuring, trading or trashing your minutes? In writing or via audio recording, track how you use the next 24 hours in detail. Then decide what time was invested or lost.

46. Ask yourself the right questions to get the right answers. Ask:

"How can I...?"
"Who do I have to be to...?"
Ask the questions with the innocence of a child, then apply the answers like an adult. ACT-I-ON!

47. "Alter my life by altering my attitude of mind." We become what we think about. Give and use your power name to your Destiny Letter Self. Say "I am now (insert your highest self name here). I think, act and feel as (name) every day." Repeat your highest self name so you can begin to identify with the best you. When you meet someone new, introduce yourself by that name and see how it feels. Do that until it feels natural. Check in with your future self. She or he is rooting for you to succeed because your decisions now are shaping the life of the future you.

48. Read your Destiny Letter (see Section Destiny-Purpose) each morning when you wake up and each evening just before you sleep. Did you notice that I keep repeating this recommendation throughout the book? What's important is worth repeating. Have you

94

been doing it? This ritual will help connect your conscious mind and subconscious mind to begin to pull you in the direction of your heart's desire. If you haven't written out your Destiny Letter, go to the number 3 of the book and do it now. It's important to bring to your awareness the versions of yourself that you want to emerge.

49. Once we make the decision to grow beyond who we currently are, it is important to get comfortable with tension between your present and future selves.

BE BOTH:

Present	--	Future
a Realist	--	a Dreamer
Practical	--	Impractical
Logical	--	Illogical

Practice accepting being uncomfortable in the dance of being in both present and future you.

PURPOSE

50. Are you still trying to rediscover the purpose you were created for? Here's one way to unearth one of your main purposes and make money with it:

-       Make a Happy column. This your list of everything you can remember that made you happy.

Think back to when you were a kid, a teen, a young optimistic adult. Allow yourself to remember all of the fun that you may have locked away or put on a shelf on your way to being "responsible".

- Highlight those items on your list that involve any kind of skill and identify that skill. Write down what that skill is.

- Make a Joy Column. Rank the top 10 chosen items in the order of joy they bring you. Whatever makes you the happiest of all gets 10 big points. This should be done from your heart, not your head. Don't filter out those "unrealistic" or "silly" things that make your heart excited.

- Make an Income Column. Now rank the top 10 highlighted items in terms of their income potential. The most lucrative skill of all is worth 10 points. If you are not sure, Google search the potential incomes from related jobs in that field.

- Total the two. The item with the highest score represents a potential main purpose in your life that can bring you joy, happiness and income.

- Develop and work on improving this skill within you. Focus all your efforts on becoming the expert in this ONE skill. Then you can add another skill or interest from your list once you master the one you choose.

But this is just one way of many to identify what you want to do next. The most important thing is to choose, and start. Like I told my daughters, you don't have to pick what you want to do for the rest of your life. That's way too much pressure. Just choose what you want to do for the next level or phase of your life.

51. HEAD + HAND + HEART = FLOW

Operating in flow is about living in that sweet spot of creativity. Your purpose, mission, goals, and even everyday tasks, when done while you're in flow will pull you through. There is little need to use willpower in order to push yourself through the task. In these next three sessions, read the following three descriptions to see how to make small 2mm adjustments to tap into your sweet spot of flow.

HEAD + HAND + HEART = FLOW

Having heart is about being aware of your unconscious motivations. Look at what you really like an prefer to do and have. What present needs are you trying to fulfill?

Need HEART? Find supportive people and tools to help you. Avoid negative self-motivation and negative self-talk. Find new motivators that stimulate and excite you. And most importantly, develop a compelling vision to help create the movie you'll play over and over again in your mind so it can infuse your heart.

52. HEAD + HAND + HEART = FLOW

Having head is about understanding clearly what you value most. Write out your goals and values and all the things in your life you find important. What future needs are you trying to fulfill?

Need HEAD? Start by increasing your commitment to your goals. Convince yourself with better arguments as to why you must get results. Talk yourself into it with new incentives to reach intermediate milestones you set. And most important, examine honestly what may be slowing you down. There are often conflicts in your goals. Ex) I want to travel the world, but I want to be at home every day. Resolve goal conflicts to open HEAD flow.

53. HEAD + HAND + HEART = FLOW

Having HAND is about being able to actually do the task. Are your skills, knowledge and abilities sufficient to deliver with massive value? Having action-relate knowledge also stimulates confidence within.

Need HAND? Find a network of people to operate within who are doing what you want to do. Find a coach, trainer, personal assistant, etc. to provide proper support. They will help you to identify blind spots that you may need to work on. They will also identify the skills you have that you may be overlooking or undervaluing.

Looking for a wonderful tribe to connect with? Check out the AWA Facebook page at https://www.facebook.com/AWA4Life

BUSINESS

54. Are you tapping into your best resource for money increase?

1)   Identify what you can do right now (skills) or what you know (information)
2)   Identify whose life might improve with access to this skill or information
3)   Increase your value to their life by providing it in exchange for money (sales)

And in case you may have forgotten, "identify" means Think about it *and* Write It Down in Your Journal.

55. "Our rewards in life will always be in exact proportion to our contribution and service."

What we earn is a mathematical equation:
$M = N + A - R$

The amount of **M**oney paid to me = the **N**eed for what I do + my **A**bility to do it - how difficult it is to **R**eplace me.

Reflect on your equation and the results you are getting now. Now map out the results you want to get and positive ways you can shift elements of your equation to increase your money results.

56. Don't allow unproductive meetings to eat up your most important and most valuable commodity - your time.

Mandate that whoever would like to have a meeting with you must first submit the following Q&A to you, in advance.

1. What is the problem?
2. What is the cause of the problem?
3. What are all of the possible solutions to the problem?
4. Which solution do you suggest?

When you or your team think first by committing these answers to writing, the need for most meetings will be eliminated. This also empowers people to take action and resolve issues.

-      based on Dale Carnegie's "How to Stop Worrying and Start Living".

57. Overcoming the fear of failure is an important skill in business and in life. When defeat comes, accept it as a signal that your plans are not sound. Make micro adjustments and set sail once more towards your coveted goal. (Napoleon Hill). "Failure is merely an opportunity to more intelligently begin again." (Henry Ford). I'd like to offer you the re-focusing mantra I use to remind me of the benefits of so-called failure:

There is no such thing as failure; there's only feedback, which makes me smarter and smarter. As a professional "failure", I will find something good - a valuable lesson - that makes me smarter next time. I recognize that my biggest problem today could be my biggest gift tomorrow.

I, therefore pronounce blessings on limitations, releasing the power of God over all things, situations and persons. I release the potential within myself, allowing this opportunity to manifest. I am grateful for this feedback.

58. Without sales, a business is just an expensive hobby. So, get comfortable with the dance of sales by looking at it from a service point of view. How can you use your special skills, services and products to make a difference for others?

When you add value to people's lives, you deserve to be paid. When you are paid, only then can you take care of yourself and your family.

By taking care of yourself and your family, you are able to think of ways to use your resources to add even more value to people's lives. They then pay you even more money. What a wonderful upward spiral of sales and service!

CONTRIBUTION AND SERVICE

59. One of the biggest shifts that I ever made in transforming my life was understanding the law of giving and receiving. It's one of the simplest, yet most underutilized opportunities. Yes, I said opportunity. Once I understood that giving is just that, I searched for smart ways to do it as much as possible.

Giving smartly means to connect with your heart and to assess with your head. You may have the desire to give good things to your kids, but handing your 5 year old the car keys is not using your head. You may have the head to give a present to the president of your company. But if you are doing it so you can get a promotion, you are not giving with your heart. So

102

smart giving encompasses two parts - a thoughtful, analytical head and a joyous, sincere heart.

Why is giving an opportunity? Because it is actually the gateway to receiving.

Think back over your life. Can you remember times that you gave anything of value and you received unexpectedly? Jot this experience down in your journal. Can you think of a time that you received from someone and suddenly you felt an overwhelming urge to give, either back to them or to pay it forward? Remember that feeling.

60. When you give love, you get to experience the feeling immediately as you give it. And then you will receive it back because you are tapping into that part of you that is a loving, caring person. Whatever we focus on always expands and grows. Even if the person or animal that you are loving on does not directly love you back, you are in the flow of energy that attracts to you from other sources.

Examine the place(s) of lack of love in your life. Write down what they are. Examine the places that you are not in lack but would like to expand or do better in love. List at least 5 ways you can give in this area. Right now, do something to commit to giving in one of these ways. Journal your decision so that it become part of your contract with yourself, and you can remember to recognize when the Universe begins to expand this part of your life.

61. Money works the same way as love. When I began tithing 10% of the gross of what I earn to my church Bethel Christian Center International in New Jersey US, which I know is doing the right things with the money in their outreach programs, things quickly began shifting for me. It actually first shifted something inside of me. No longer did that feeling of not having enough money haunt me. I gave and still somehow managed to have enough to pay my bills. But then debts I owed started being forgiven. Things I wanted to buy were given to me for free or at a discount. I got raises at work. So what I learned is that there is financial abundance.

Examine the place(s) of lack of money in your life. Write down what they are. Examine the places that you are not in lack but would like to expand or do better in money. List at least 5 ways you can give in this area. Right now, do something to commit to giving in one of these ways. Journal your decision so that it become part of your contract with yourself, and you can remember to recognize when the Universe begins to expand this part of your life.

62. I started looking for ways to give in other ways. I donate my time to coach people through certain organizations and volunteer to speak to members of charities to share what I've learned about how to really make life amazing. And then my time expanded. Opportunities to partner with amazing people presented themselves so I could do more, do it better, in less time.

Examine the place(s) of lack of time in your life. Write down what they are. Examine the places that you are not in lack but would like to expand or to have more time to do better. List at least 5 ways you can give in this area. Right now, do something to commit to giving in one of these ways. Journal your decision so that it become part of your contract with yourself, and you can remember to recognize when the Universe begins to expand this part of your life.

I am so excited for you. As you give into the collective Oneness of the Universe in any way, you will get back what you are giving out, only magnified and multiplied. But this works for good things or bad things we do. So be sure to give good, smart from your head *and* lovingly from your heart.

CHAPTER 5: HIGHER HABITAT – Loving the Only Place You Live In

FOOD

63. Focusing on eating plant-based foods are an important tool in the alignment to your most energetic self.

The action of being deliberate in your thoughts about yourself, your life, the people in your life, and what's truly important to you brings you into the center of your highest, most perfect self. By treating your body, your mind and your spirit with the love and care you have shown it in this process, you are now opening the pathway to live in abundant energy. And the results are transformative - peace, clarity, energy, joy, health, strength, and of course, love.

It's pure, positive energy! It's the place where your hopes, your dreams and your true self are waiting for you.

Go into your kitchen and see how many live foods are present there. If not a lot, go get them now and look up recipes in the book <u>Fork Disease! Go Vegan!</u> and in many other sources on how to use them as a part of your daily eating. You don't have to eat 100% vegan to make a real difference for yourself.

64. If you do choose to eat vegan, becoming a socially friendly vegan is good for everyone. "Friendly" is the key word here, not vegan.

Eating can be a private, wonderful experience for one, or an intimate dinner for two. But more often than not, eating is social, communal, to be shared with friends and family, talking and laughing. And of course, there are holidays, anniversaries and birthdays. No matter what the important event, food often takes center stage.

Choosing a vegan lifestyle does not mean you have to live as a recluse at home alone. Go out with friends and family, and be bold – ask for what you want. Vegan substitutions are more likely to be available at restaurants that make food to order. Ask if it's okay to substitute foods for health reasons.

As you embrace this plant-based lifestyle with family and friends, your non-mainstream choices for eating may be challenged, even by strangers. But stay patient and celebrate yourself for not being "normal". Normal leads to sickness and disease. Being the renegade that you are, you will enjoy health and energy. You don't have to be militant about this. RELAX and enjoy your transformational eating journey, and whatever that means for you. Don't worry about putting labels on yourself.

Go online and examine 5 different restaurant menus for plant-based (vegan) options. Look at different types of cuisine that you already like. Now you are expanding your awareness of what is there. You can go out with family, friends and co-workers and select plant-based options for yourself without making a big deal out of it. So go out and enjoy yourself!

65. *Milk...from Plants?* The thought of changing eating habits you've had since childhood may seem scary. We understand because we went through the exact same thing. We grew up eating just about everything that walked, flew, swam or had parents. So you can imagine that for us, choosing to switch to motherless plant-based milk at first seemed unimaginable. Now it's just the opposite. We rarely drink milk meant for a calf or other animal. We now primarily choose almond, rice, coconut, nut, soy, oat, flax or hemp milk over cow's milk.

Go buy one of the plant-based milks and drink it for this week. Then when that is done, try a different one. They are usually located right next to the cow's milk in the supermarket.

66. Focus on flavors, not flesh. As health coaches, we are often asked the question – "So just how do I transition to eating more of a whole-foods, plant-based diet? Do I have to give up everything I love to eat?" We want to answer this question right here, because the answer is simple. NO! You don't have to give up all of those wonderful flavors you love.

Focus on a lifestyle of eating "well" – meaning eating delicious meals that support your health. By applying the spices you used on meats instead to hearty vegetables, you are now learning about new and exciting foods to expand your palate.

Use Fork Disease! Go Vegan! as a roadmap to the healthy lifestyle you desire, paved with the flavors you already love!

Look at the spices in your pantry and the sauces in your refrigerator that you might normally use on meat. Add it to a vegetable and savor the new combination of heath and familiar delicious flavor.

67. *PLANT-BASED LIVING - 21 DAYS TO FREEDOM.* Why do we recommend beginning your journey with 21 days of plant-based eating? Did you know that after 21 days, the seeds are planted within your spirit, and your brain has begun to register that something is shifting? Your brain will begin to seek this out as your new "normal" routine.

Deciding to make a lifestyle change is only the first, albeit important, step. However, sticking to it long enough for the changes to register and take root is important for long-term results.

But do not be fooled. 21 days only toils the ground and plants the seeds. The complete habit, like enjoying the fruit of the tree, takes dedication, love and patience.

Basically, focusing on 21 days of plant-based eating lays the groundwork to create a stronger connection to your self-image as a healthy, food-enjoying, exercising, happier person.

EXERCISE

68. Exercise to move into your best body. Exercise helps us lose weight and keep it off. It reduces our appetite for unhealthy foods, normalizes blood sugar and lowers cholesterol. Our stress levels decrease while our energy and concentration ability increases. And we get to live in a muscular, toned, strong, sexy body too!

Now, it's time to accelerate your journey to living in your higher energy! For the next 21 days, decide to exercise - and then actually DO IT. Write down your daily exercise progress in your eating journal. You'll be amazed at your success over this short time.

But don't make it complicated. You don't need new workout clothes, a gym membership that never gets used, or expensive equipment to get results. Look on YouTube or Google search for simple body exercises like sit-ups, push-ups, leg lifts, jumping jacks, wall-sits, and speed walking for just 30-45 minutes a day, you'll achieve amazing results! Grab a friend or loved one and go for a walk, then increase the speed and distance. Put on your favorite music and get to it!

69. Examine your body-weight exercises that you have selected. *Build Up Daily While Celebrating Each Day.* Set a goal of how many repetitions you want to complete for each exercise and then challenge yourself to do it.

Begin gradually, with 5 or 10 repetitions. Then take a break for a minute. Do it again, building up your strength by just doing what you can. Then add a few more repetitions every day until 30 minutes have passed.

No matter how many you have done for that day, congratulate yourself! This is the most important part of exercising. Your brain will begin to associate good feelings with what you just accomplished, release endorphins, and then you'll begin to want to do it more and more.

70. *Developing Your Workout Rituals.* In developing what gets you going, make bite-sized rituals that you can incorporate easily. If possible, workout at the same time each day. And remember, "as the mind goes, so will the body".

How we think, what we focus on, and what we say will eventually manifest into what we see in the mirror and how we feel inside. Be prepared with your phrases of positive, encouraging words to keep you exercising. By using our natural process of alignment between body movement, positive thoughts, and great eating, we achieve amazing results that will last a lifetime.

Find your favorite upbeat, positive language song. Put it on as loud as you can, to really feel the beats. Smile. Bigger smile while you are enjoying the music. Now dance. Moving your body to your favorite song while smiling actually benefits your mind, body and soul. You can add this to your workout rituals. Yes, it still counts if it's fun.

71. Reframe what you think exercise "must" be in order to "count". Merriam-Webster Dictionary has many definitions for the word "exercise". And none of them are negative. It speaks about exercise as a noun in which you engage in "the act of bringing into play or realizing in action". Maybe you can reframe exercise as PLAY!

They also define exercise as "the act...of carrying out the terms of an agreement". Maybe you can reframe exercise as saying YES! to being active.

There's also a definition of "regular or repeated use of a faculty or bodily organ" and "bodily exertion for the sake of developing and maintaining physical fitness". Maybe for all of you consenting adults, you can add more energetic SEX! to your definition of exercise. See, it can be fun!

The dictionary also includes the definition "something performed or practiced in order to develop, improve, or display a specific capability or skill". How about adding SPORTS! to your exercise options?

There's a definition of "a maneuver, operation, or drill carried out for training and discipline". Discipline is about setting boundaries and making decisions for what you want and don't want, and can be a form of self-love. Let's reframe exercise as LOVE!

So, what is exercise?

SAYING YES TO BEING ACTIVE! Choose to engage in responsible PLAY! SEX! SPORTS! SELF-LOVE!

Remember, your outcome is not to exercise, but to be healthier, more energetic and happier in your body. So jot down 10 ways you can easily accomplish this. Now you have many ways to choose from every day for variety and in case circumstances of life get in the way of an option.

SELF-PRESERVATION

72. Practice focusing on the perfectness of who you already are – healthy, whole and loved. There is nothing wrong with you.

We know you may have been told differently by parents, teachers, friends, media, commercials, and most of the world. Even our own inner voice began to believe the lies and repeat them – reminding us of the things we've fallen short of, failed in, and telling us what we "can't" become. Our inner voice was hypnotized into believing that those lies were truth, and in so believing, we made them manifest.

As we de-hypnotize ourselves through applying the things in this book, our inner voice will shift to become our biggest champion. The real you will emerge more and more – the you that is a joyous, generous spirit. The real you, confident, of a peaceful mind with a strong, healthy body, will become the norm.

"There is a force within which gives you life - Seek that.

In your body lies a priceless gem –Seek that.

If you want to find the greatest treasure,
Don't look outside, Look inside, and Seek that."
----Rumi

Look into your mirror. Look into your own eyes. Look deeper into your soul. Smile at yourself - you are a lovely person. Now, even if this feels strange or uncomfortable, say aloud, "I love you." Receive the love you are giving to you. Every time you look into a mirror, give this precious gift to yourself.

73. *Share your Journey When People are Ready.* You'll be so excited at the changes you are experiencing as you move in life-affirming habits and watch the old ones fade away. And in that excitement, you may want to share what you've learned with EVERYONE.

But pause for a moment. Mental and emotional openness is necessary for each of us to transition in any area of our lives to another echelon of being. You'll know when someone is receptive. They'll engage you in a positive way, asking questions - and you'll feel their excited, curious energy.

These are the people that you can share your knowledge and love of these recipes to a successful life with. Otherwise, just enjoy their company, and wait for them to ask you about the wonderful new you they are seeing. Then, share away!

Is there anyone in your life that is noticing and asking about the shifts in you?

74. *Know your Why… and Review it Regularly.* You may experience several mental and emotional shifts as you work to create your best self. In the beginning, you might find it very easy if you are truly inspired and understand your "Why".

Jumping in fully by doing the suggestions in this book and keeping a journal of your answers will help you to become clear on your goals and the reasons why you want to transition in your abundant lifestyle. Expect to be excited and empowered, especially as you grow to feel better, stronger and more energetic all around.

Today, review your previous steps in this book and your journal record. Are there any shifts you are having difficulty implementing? Is there anything that feels like you are pushing yourself to do or that you are resisting doing? It's often a result of your "why not" being defined in a stronger way that is frightening you.

List your reasons why instead, and make them exciting, important, passionate, real reasons that matter to you. By doing this "why" list, you will begin to feel pulled into your new activities. Operating in the flow of pulling energy is way easier, and more fun.

75. *Take Purpose Breaks.* Make time each day to DO NOTHING. Yes, you are going to schedule your "lazy times". We've been trained to see the things we do and acknowledge them as valuable. But many of us have never been taught to also celebrate when we take our breaks. I used to feel guilty whenever I blew off a project to watch a movie, or chatted with a friend about nothing when I "should" be taking care of something else, or when I just wanted to lay on the couch for a nap. But this is valuable downtime, at least when we do it without guilt. But constant pushing often leads to burn-out, depression, discontentment, and resentment.

By scheduling time each day to be still, to surrender to the flow of life, to be aware of the present, to sit still, to breathe deeply, to meditate, to have mindless time, or just to do NOTHING, it changes your emotions around it. You don't feel guilty because you allotted this time to what you are doing (or not doing). You protect yourself from doing too much nothing and not getting done what you have on your agenda because you have decided ahead of time your end time.

What is the purpose of these breaks? These acts release the pressure valve that you are under, allows your mind, body and spirit to rejuvenate, and brings you into a grateful space of peace.

And the surprise is that your energy and focus will increase when you go back into your actions, and you'll feel happier while doing them!

Schedule yourself a purpose break into your day today. And just relax. Chill out. It'll be ok.

BODY CARE

76. *GREAT HABITS ARE FORMED DAILY.* Most people want positive habits to immediately be as easy as brushing their teeth. But the reality is being great isn't always easy. In fact, greatness requires sacrifice. It requires doing things that others won't or can't do.

Truth be told, good habits require consistent commitment.

Highly successful people have learned to develop good habits. Make the commitment to make it past the internal resistance, no matter how many times you need to "start again", to reach new levels of success.

Even when you mess up, and you will, remember, you are never really starting over. So don't "throw the baby out with the bathwater" as the saying goes. You are continuing on your journey with more experience and hopefully more understanding of what works and does not work for you, and where you need to adjust for better results. And one day you'll realize that your empowering actions are habits that come as easily as brushing your teeth!

Today is about forgiving yourself for your "mistakes", "failures", and "cheats" on your journey of caring for yourself at a higher level. So get back to your mirror. Look into your eyes and say "I forgive you. I celebrate all the times you did well and forgive the times you made a different choice. Now, today, I support you on making empowering choices. I love you."

77. Today is a free choice day for you! (Secret: they are all free choice days). If you could do something to show love and care for your body, what will you choose to do today that supports your dreams, hopes and best version of the physical you? Put on a beautiful or handsome outfit from your closet and go grocery shopping? Treat yourself to a massage or pedicure? Walk barefoot through the grass and enjoy the sunshine on your face?

78. *Take out the Trash!* You are working hard to achieve and maintain your physical health at optimal levels. The best way to begin is usually to move out the old stuff. Detoxing at some level as part of your lifestyle will help. You don't have to do a detox for an extended period to gain benefits. There are many ways to detox, and you can ideally do it for 3 – 5 days, or even just one day. Once every few months would be great for a longer fast (8 – 14 days).

Are you ready to clean out your body right now? We recommend you be gentle with yourself by beginning with a detox for 1 -3 days. Just do what you can, and celebrate yourself for your effort and successes. We will be celebrating right along with you!

79. *Are you Watering Yourself?* This base level of flushing your system should become a regular part of your life. Drink plain water regularly. If you followed the guidance in this book, and incorporated lots of water as a regular part of your lifestyle, the difference will be amazing!

Who would've thought that something as basic as water was the answer to what ails us all along?

Dehydration actually produces pain and many degenerative diseases, including asthma, arthritis, hypertension, angina, adult-onset diabetes, lupus and multiple sclerosis. Dr. Batmanghelidj message to the world is, "You are not sick, you are thirsty. Don't treat thirst with medication."

How much water? The minimum amount of water to drink daily is "your body weight divided by 2 = minimum number of ounces per day".

For example, if you weigh 160 pounds / 2 = 80 ounces. The average size water bottle is 16 oz. = 5 bottles. (72 kilograms / 2 = 2.4 liters). If you're not used to drinking plain water, it may seem like a lot. One trick is to put a bottle by your bedside and drink it as soon as you wake up.

This will get your system started the right way, and you'll crave more water throughout the day. Keep your bottle of water with you throughout the day. You'll suddenly find yourself staring at the bottom of your empty bottle wondering "Who drank all of my water?"

Pick out a special water bottle that makes you feel special. Do you see one in your favorite color or with a cool design? Get it and enjoy it all day long.

80. *Read For A Healthier Body.* Get in the habit of reading the labels on food packages as you shop. As you learn to decipher what the ingredients on the labels are, you will feel more empowered. You will be able to quickly recognize what to avoid.

Perhaps you can even take the advice I gave to my then six-year old: If you can't read it, don't eat it.

She has easily made more sensible food choices in the supermarket ever since. With knowledge comes empowerment.

Understanding what is in food and what those strange words actually mean, will provide you with selective buying power.

Read the ingredient labels on each item in your pantry or cupboard. If you don't recognize a word, look it up immediately to find out what it is. Now decide consciously if you want to eat those ingredients. Decide if you want to buy that item again or if you want to choose something else next time.

81. *Is it Morning? Celebrate with a Cold Shower.* This may not be what you want to read, and trust me, I understand. I hate being cold. But giving our body the gift of a cold shower or bath works wonders! It reduces inflammation in joints, increases blood circulation, and really wakes you up. Your hair and skin will appear more radiant, and even stimulates weight loss. It also eases stress and relieves depression symptoms.

I began this process by washing my face in cold water in the mornings. I then added it to my neck. Then I began cool water rinses in the tub, beginning at my feet, and working my way up. Day by day, I made the water cooler. Then I started stepping into the cool running shower, and reduced the temperature a little bit each day. Or you can be bold and just plunge right into a cold shower, bath or pool! I've only done this a couple of times, but I know people who do this every day. Wild!

The important thing is to allow your body this simple, free, all-around body care.

Top 10 Things that May Dismiss your Dreams, Decisions and Destiny

Congratulations! You have just entered the 1% of people in the world that took specific action to learn and apply the One Law. Like drinking water, eating food, and sleeping, this is an ever-evolving process. My suggestion is to revisit your journal that you've created regularly, make micro-adjustments to your choices, and keep strengthening your vision of who you really are, why you are here, and what you are truly capable of. But we can't only focus on the flowers.

As motivational speaker Jim Rohn said, we have to also be aware of the weeds. If we don't constantly pull up the weeds while we are planting the flowers, the weeds will take over your garden.

As an attorney, I was well aware that there were many reasons that a court would dismiss a case. So, I had to prepare my case to the best of my ability in order to prevent this from happening. Right now, you are about create your case for your best life. In listening to a talk by Bishop T.D. Jakes, Dedication 2 Destiny, January 5, 2020, I was inspired by what I heard and adapted the information into the below Top 10 List to help you to make sure that the Universe doesn't dismiss your case for your abundant life.

1. Dreaming too small, or not at all (did you do your Destiny Letter, in action step 3? Is it truly everything that your heart desires?)
2. Being unspecific about what you want (vs. S.M.A.R.T. goals - specific, measurable, actionable, realistic, time-defined)
3. Not measuring your life (dates, amounts, numbers, with who, micro-steps, scheduled times)

4. Going after things not in alignment with your destiny – choose "great" over "good" (say no to good, say yes and dedicate yourself to great and outstanding)

5. Carrying dead weight, unforgiveness, anger, negativity, guilt, suffering (let it go, let it go, let it go…)

6. The language you choose to use (what you say and how you say it matters - your subconscious is always listening to you for your commands).

7. The things you choose to focus on (are you seeing all of the amazing things in your life to be grateful for and what you've done right, or are you only seeing what you perceive as wrong?)

8. Being in environments of people and places that drain you (you are not a tree permanently planted, so leave).

9. Not protecting and dictating your time (yes, you have control over this - it is limited to 24 hours a day, so value it).

10. Being inconsistent between what you want and how you consistently live (it takes time to change habits, so be patient with yourself, keep going).

CONCLUSION

In the next 1-5 years, the world will be changing dramatically. In 10 years, you will be truly in awe. This is nothing to fear. It is an opportunity to adapt your views of what is possible so that you can fully embrace all of the possibilities in you. As new technology emerges, Artificial Intelligence frees up our time, solar, wind, and nuclear energies replace current options, health advances enable us to live longer, preventative options replaces current medicine, as the world currencies shifts how we do business, as our imaginations of artificial borders of countries and allies are realigned, as current professions are replaced with new ones - remember the One Law.

In this understanding, there is nothing to fear. We are one energy, ever growing and evolving. We can never be separate, unloved, or alone except if we create the imaginings and live in that. The truth is that we are one cosmic heartbeat, always creating abundance in whatever we choose, in any circumstances. With your new insights from The One Law, look forward 10 years from now. Perhaps re-read and adjust your letter to you from your future self to reflect even more expansive possibilities.

If you'd like to live your amazing, abundant life, much faster, I'd love to help you get there. As your coach, cheerleader and accountability partner, I help you spot the weeds while planting your flowers. This is an amazing New World Order you are entering into. Be amazed. Be amazing. As the song goes, "You've got what it takes."

Celebrate Your Progress, Big and Small! Take a moment and congratulate yourself for being where you are right now. This is always either your moment of change, or the moment just before your moment of change. This is why you have used this book.

Continue on your journey of applying the One Law. I encourage you to begin right where you are today, which is the only way to get to the tomorrow you desire. Even if you are not ready to apply all of this information in this book, do what feels best for you, and apply a little more each day. But we suspect, because you have read this far, you have already made amazing transformations in living your Amazing Abundant life now! Congratulations!

Reach out to me at www.AWA4Life.com. I am here for you.

With all the loving light of the universe to you,
Marjah

Free Templates offered at www.AWA4Life.com:

- Free Journal Page template (#2 Create Good Habits)
- Contract for Success Template (#3 Destiny Letter)
- 10 Year Action Celebration Tool (#6 Lean in the Dream)
- Weekly Intentions Guide (#8 Set Your Intentions)
- Purpose Discovery Blueprint (#50 Purpose)